THE SUBTLETY OF
GEORGE BERNARD SHAW

BOOKS BY PATRICK BRAYBROOKE

CRITICISM

G. K. Chesterton.
Some Thoughts on Hilaire Belloc.
J. M. Barrie.
Lord Morley.
Considerations on Edmund Gosse.
The Genius of Bernard Shaw.
Kipling and his Soldiers.
Thomas Hardy and his Philosophy.
Some Aspects of H. G. Wells.
The Wisdom of G. K. Chesterton.

ESSAYS

Novelists we are Seven.
Some Goddesses of the Pen.
Peeps at the Mighty.
Philosophies in Modern Fiction.
Great Children in Literature.

NOVELS

Cruelty.
The Man who Arrived.

ANTHOLOGIES

A Chesterton Catholic Anthology.
A Child's Robert Louis Stevenson.

MISCELLANEOUS

Oddments.
Suggestive Fragments.
The Short Story : How to write it.

In Preparation :

A Child's Charles Dickens
[Foreword by Walter Dexter
—Editor of *The Dickensian*].
The Art of John Galsworthy.

THE SUBTLETY OF
GEORGE BERNARD SHAW

by

PATRICK BRAYBROOKE, F.R.S.L.
Member of the Fabian Society

HASKELL HOUSE PUBLISHERS Ltd.
Publishers of Scarce Scholarly Books
NEW YORK, N. Y. 10012
1973

HASKELL HOUSE PUBLISHERS Ltd.

Publishers of Scarce Scholarly Books

280 LAFAYETTE STREET

NEW YORK. N. Y. 10012

Library of Congress Cataloging in Publication Data

Braybrooke, Patrick, 1894-
  The subtlety of George Bernard Shaw.

  Bibliography: p.
  1. Shaw, George Bernard, 1856-1950. I. Title.
PR5367.B73 1973   822'.9'12   72-2125
ISBN 0-8383-1465-1

Printed in the United States of America

DEDICATION

My dear Rossi,

I do not agree with you. You are right and I am wrong. That is why I do not agree with you.
Yours affectionately,
PATRICK BRAYBROOKE.

The Reverend ARTHUR ROSSI BRAYBROOKE,
Cotswold,
Stroud,
Gloucestershire.

AUTHOR'S NOTE

WITHOUT a shadow of doubt Bernard Shaw is the greatest figure in the English Theatre in this early twentieth century. His genius is amazing, his subtlety is genius. Shaw is great enough to be quite frequently wrong in his deductions. He is great enough to be right when the majority of men are wrong. Shaw has one great weakness. He cannot laugh at himself, so sometimes the critics have to do it for him. Shaw has written several plays which reach the pinnacle of genius ; he has written none which fall very far short of it.

This book deals with a few aspects of Bernard Shaw. Those aspects of his art and thought which seemed most interesting and most typical have been selected. The day will come when we shall need an epitaph for Bernard Shaw. Perhaps it might be : " Through his life he hit men because he loved them. Through his life he chastised their bodies that in the day of God their souls might appear white and spotless."

PATRICK BRAYBROOKE.

70, Gloucester Street, LONDON, S.W.1.
Winter, 1929.

CONTENTS

Part I

THE WISDOM OF G. K. CHESTERTON

By PATRICK BRAYBROOKE

7/6 net

SOME PRESS OPINIONS

" Mr. Braybrooke's book is obviously the fruit of detailed and conscientious study of his subject."—*The Daily Telegraph*.

" The book as a whole makes very good reading."—*Nottingham Guardian*.

" An interesting and thoughtful study in literary criticism."—*The Scotsman*.

" It is a service to the world—nothing like quite the same thing has been done before, not even by Shaw."—*The Times of India*.

" He is the man for the job."—*The Tablet*.

" It will enhance a reputation that is already justifiably well established."—*Edinburgh Evening News*.

A CHILD'S R. L. STEVENSON

COMPILED BY PATRICK BRAYBROOKE

7/6 net

SOME PRESS OPINIONS

" Its subject and the names of its author and publisher will be sufficient guarantee of its quality and chance of success."—*The Newsagent*.

" A very skilful introduction to the great writer."—*The Publisher and Bookseller*.

" The numerous well chosen selections."—*Edinburgh Evening News*.

" Brilliant."—*The Bookman*.

NOVELS BY PATRICK BRAYBROOKE, 7/6 each

CRUELTY

" A tale which is told with much skill."—*The Scotsman*.

" A sincere and painstaking piece of work."—*Times Literary Supplement*.

" It is stimulating and provocative."—*Newcastle Chronicle*.

THE MAN WHO ARRIVED

" A story with charm."—*Liverpool Courier*.

" —— a novel into which have been woven some of the most wonderfully human characters portrayed for some time."—*Dundee Courier*.

x

PART I

Chapter I

TWO EARLY PLAYS

IN starting his career as a playwright Bernard Shaw made no apology for using the theatre as a means of a distinct attack. Shaw respected the theatre in the sense that he thought it a proper vehicle to carry his message about people who were not specially respectable. He did not deal with villains : he dealt with humbugs. He knew that his shafts would pierce their self-complacency, while he knew equally well that his shafts would simply ricochet off pure and undefiled scoundrels. Shaw hit at people who pretended to be a little less evil than they were. He was tired of writing novels which the publishers were too tired to publish. He was rather bored by knowing exactly what to expect by the morning post. He asked himself not only " What is wrong with my novels," but also " What is wrong with the world," and he asked himself yet again " What is wrong with the theatre ? " He found that his novels were wrong because they were simply not novels : he found the world was wrong because it had been made in six days and refused to rest on the seventh : he found that the theatre was wrong because it had not tried his own plays. The result of the sum of these thinkings was *Widowers' Houses*.

Widowers' Houses caused a sensation in London,

which meant that one person in a hundred thousand heard about it and that ninety per cent. of the dramatic critics passed a first night in a state of unusual mental activity. As Bernard Shaw said at the time, " he had achieved an uproar if he had not achieved success." He has, of course, achieved a successful uproar all his life.

Widowers' Houses concerns a problem in which Shaw is always interested. It is the problem that has to do with the income that we derive from dividends. Now there are a very large number of people who would be extremely surprised if they were told that they were taking part in evil and tyranny. They would, no doubt, search their own lives, to find them clear of objectionable scars. And yet it would come as a painful surprise and shock to them if they realised that the money they obtained from their dividends was the result of sweating and possibly direct immorality.

Widowers' Houses is a clash between a rather sensible scamp and a rather foolish and yet well-meaning idealist who has the courage of his convictions so long as he is not likely to be severely conflicted by them. Sartorius, the unscrupulous landlord, generally manages to make a good case for himself. Trench, the idealist, quite often manages to make a good case against himself.

Trench wishes to marry Blanche Sartorius, but does not wish to benefit by his potential father-in-law's income. Blanche, on the other hand, does not intend to marry Trench if the marriage means a divorce from all participation in her father's money. Such is the charming little deadlock when Shaw turns round and deals Trench a back-hander. Trench discovers also that his own dividends are derived from quite a questionable source. The result is that Trench loses his ideals, as most of us do, when money is concerned. Such, then, is the bare outline of *Widowers' Houses*.

The main interest in this early Shavian play is the evidence afforded in it of Shaw's remarkable grasp of human nature even in the days when he was merely an experimentalist in the art of the theatre. Sartorius is an excellently conceived character. He is a self-made man and, true to his type, he does not wish to be reminded of it by people who would insult him not by insults, but by politeness. Thus, when Sartorius has a fatherly conversation with Trench regarding his engagement with Blanche, we find that the landlord must be quite certain that Trench's aristocratic relations will not treat his daughter with that kindly patronage that is tolerable in royalty and intolerable in aristocracy. Trench, with all the inconsequential enthusiasm of the newly accepted lover, cannot see that the question of his relations and their attitude to Blanche has anything to do with the question of their marriage. Sartorius soon smashes up this delusion.

SARTORIUS. Excuse me, sir ; they have a great deal to do with it. I am resolved that my daughter shall approach no circle in which she will not be received with the full consideration to which her education and her breeding—I say, her breeding —entitle her.

A minor character and yet one of major importance to the problem of the play is Lickcheese. Lickcheese is Sartorius's collector of rents and is a clever Shavian character. Life has been for him a more or less perpetual illusion and he has no delusions left about it. He will not stand being brought to task by Trench, for he can rightly turn round and tell Trench that he is, in reality, just as bad, for, if Lickcheese collects the rent from ill-housed people, Trench collects his dividends from the same ill-housed people. So we get the Shavian position—that it is as well to be perfectly without sin before casting the first stone. Here, then, are some delightful lines of dialogue with Shaw in that mood of his when he shows that we, who are without blame, are not by any means outside blame. Trench is arguing with Lickcheese concerning the morality of collecting rents from householders when quite often the house scarcely holds together.

> TRENCH. I will not. It's a damnable business from beginning to end ; and you deserve no better luck for helping in it. I've seen it all among the out-patients at the hospital ; and it used to make my blood boil to think that such things couldn't be prevented.
> LICKCHEESE. Oh, indeed, sir. But I suppose you'll take your share when you marry Miss Blanche all the same. Which of us is the worse, I should like to know—me that wrings the money out to keep a home over my children, or you that spend it and try to shove the blame on to me ?

In this play Shaw manages to bring the " play-long " clash between Trench and Sartorius to a reasonable climax. Trench, with a perfectly sincere but nevertheless thoughtless enthusiasm for the right, accuses Sartorius point blank of beastly treatment of his squalid and wretched tenants. So Trench shouts an accusation at Sartorius. He shouts with all the enthusiasm of a man of rather limited intelligence who, having seen three quarters of a problem, forgets that the fourth quarter is always the most illusive of solution. With a grand show of self-righteousness Sartorius demands that he is a self-made man, which statement saves us the blasphemy of suggesting that he was made by God.

> TRENCH. You are nothing of the sort. I found out this morning from your man—Lickcheese, or whatever his confounded name is—that your fortune has been made out of a parcel of unfortunate creatures that have hardly enough to keep body and soul together—made by screwing, and bullying, and driving, and all sorts of pettifogging tyranny.

The answer given by Sartorius to this accusation is a popular answer given by those who are not of necessity blackguards. It is the answer that the poor prefer poor houses because they are too poor even to know how to keep their houses respectable. It is the answer which demands that the poor will break their necks in walking down stairs because the family on the preceding Sunday afternoon has roasted chestnuts at the admirable fire helped by the addition of the landlord's new banisters. I do not think in detail

B

the argument to be a true one, but I do think that
Shaw would have us believe that poor houses are not
so much resented by the poor as nearly poor houses
by the poor who are respectable in the sense that
they have an equality with the rich in the really
perfectly unimportant question of birth. It is, of
course, just after this discussion when Sartorius
alleges the poor to be indifferent to their surroundings,
that he hurls his bombshell at Trench by asking him
quite bluntly from what source he obtains his income.
And, as I have said, Trench discovers that his own
income comes from the collection of rents from bad
slum property and, the problem coming straight home
to him, he shelves it and passes by on his way to
collect his probable quarterly cheque.

.   .   .   .   .   .

Blanche Sartorius is excellently drawn. She has a
mind of her own and has no intention whatever of
being bothered by Trench's ridiculous scruples. If
Trench thinks Blanche is going to go without her
father's allowance he is greatly mistaken. Blanche is
willing enough to be led to the altar, but she is not
willing to be led into poverty just because Trench has
scruples about taking money that might have been
given to putting new cisterns in houses for people
who would think it quite absurd to wash in a bath
when they had paid several shillings for the kitchen
pail.

Lickcheese is a wretched little drone who can only
afford to keep his wife and children by shutting his
eyes to the fact that he is acquiescing in a good deal

of villainy. He has sufficient brains to be able to be rude artistically, and he has sufficient brains to pierce the depth of the shallowness of Trench.

In *Widowers' Houses* Shaw has looked at human nature and found that it is bad and unashamed, that it is also good as long as the being good does not create a state of material loss. " We are not humbugs," says Shaw. " We will walk up to Calvary so long as the Cross remains back in the City of Jerusalem."

.   .   .   .   .   .

In *The Philanderer* Bernard Shaw is in a jocular mood. He is having a little bit of fun and is much too unselfish to keep it all to himself. *The Philanderer* is a very mild sex play, a very faint fore-shadowing of part of *Man and Superman*. In *Widowers' Houses* Shaw found his feet : in spite of the success of that play he managed to keep his head. As though relenting at having chivied the public in *Widowers' Houses* Shaw, in *The Philanderer*, though still concerned with a problem, concerned himself with a much less desperate one. Trench is a fool because he cannot see beyond his own nose. Charteris is a fool because he can see beyond his own nose but does not derive any benefit thereby. Charteris puddles about through life, first into one mock pool of tears and then into another. He appears to love all women equally badly, while the one woman he would love quite well quite naturally objects to being merely the probable end of a queue. Grace Tranfield, who, I feel, really does like Charteris sufficiently to risk seeing him in pyjamas in the early morning not as her lover but as her husband, will not take the risk, as she happens to be that most odious thing in the world—a strong-minded woman. The plot of this pleasant " un-pleasant play " simply does not exist. The play is a study of a man who philanders through life, a doctor who philanders with medicine, a woman who is sensible enough to philander with Charteris, and another woman who is foolish enough to imagine that his philandering may one day cease so that he becomes the proud possessor of an abominable villa at Streatham.

When Shaw wrote *The Philanderer* the influence of Ibsen had spread to London and people who knew nothing about him whatever enjoyed talking about his wickedness, and with English complacency de-lighted in the fact that they were not like the magni-ficent Norwegian playwright who found in his exile from his own country a close companionship with the god of genius.

Shaw in *The Philanderer* jokes quite good-naturedly about this Ibsen cult. There is in this play the Ibsen club. Apparently the Ibsen club is a distinct fore-runner of most of the literary clubs of to-day, in which men look effeminate and women are seldom worth looking at. Thus Charteris explains the constitution of the Ibsen club. It is Shaw tilting not at eccen-tricity but at the kind of eccentricity which thinks it must attach itself to anything which is intellectual, and gathers to itself a number of superficial people.

CHARTERIS. Every candidate for membership must

be nominated by a man and a woman, who both guarantee that the candidate, if a female, is not womanly, and if male, is not manly.

At the end of Act I Charteris explains the whole muddle he is in. It is the key-note to his unsatisfactory and shallow character.

> CHARTERIS. I tell you, seriously, I'm the matter. Julia wants to marry me : I want to marry Grace. I came here to-night to sweetheart Grace. Enter Julia. Alarums and excursions. Exit Grace. Enter you and Craven. Subterfuges and excuses. Exeunt Craven and Julia. And here we are. That's the whole story. Sleep over it. Good night.

. . . . . .

Apart from Shaw's study of Charteris *The Philanderer* is peculiarly interesting to us as foreshadowing, by means of a subtle joke, the definite and heavy attack on doctors which is to be found in *The Doctor's Dilemma*. I am not sure whether Shaw is quite fair to Dr. Paramore. Dr. Paramore is by no means heartless. He is possessed of the kind of scientific mind which really quite sincerely does not grasp that disease is never science but the failure of science. That is where Shaw laughs derisively at Dr. Paramore. Dr. Paramore is naturally disappointed to find that the disease upon which he has been working is not a disease at all. Paramore (and who could not be sorry for him?) feels that he has wasted much time and energy. We do him a vast injustice if we think him to be callous, without a spark of humanity. It is true that Paramore calls the good news of the absence of his disease bad news, but I feel it is very important in fairness to him to emphasise the fact that the non-existence of this disease is bad news to him because it means the end of a possibility of establishing him as an original medical thinker. The absence of the disease robs Paramore of a name even while it really adds to the sum of scientific benefit. Paramore, when it comes to the vital point, is a brave enough person. He will admit that he diagnosed Colonel Craven's disease quite wrongly for the simple reason that he attributed to him a disease which did not find immortality by being included in every general prac-titioner's manual of medicine.

The argument between Colonel Craven and Dr. Paramore concerning the question of cruelty cannot be answered merely by saying it is the inevitable clash of the man who is cruel for science and the man who is cruel for sport. So far does Shaw go. There is the kind of see-saw argument between Craven and Paramore—Craven upbraiding Paramore for the use of vivisection, Paramore retorting, not exactly logically, " Well, my dear fellow, what about fox-hunting ? " At this point the argument in the play breaks off. It breaks off just when we feel Shaw ought to have let it go on. It is the curse of the theatre. An argument cannot be anything else but superficial, something must happen, a jug must fall or a door must bang, or the audience will melt into the street and pass away in a succession of taxi-cabs. For the problem of vivisection is not in the least a question of whether it is cruel. It is abominably cruel. The human being who is saved by vivisection saves his body and damns his soul. The case against vivisection is that it is always the wrong means to a right end. Bernard Shaw, as I say, in the interests of the theatre leaves off the argument at the critical point. He continues it all through his philosophy, that most excellent philosophy which has as its central teaching the Life Force idea. The substitute for vivisection is not non-vivisection, but mankind learning to live properly. Vivisection is a blasphemous lie: disease is a blasphemous lie. We accept vivisection because we accept disease as being inevitable. In *The Philanderer* Shaw admits that vivisection is cruel. That does not, perhaps, really matter. What does matter is that scientific medical men believe their work to be useful and beneficial when, as a matter of fact, it is merely an example of an inevitable necessity.

To get back to the main argument in this play, the simple philandering of Charteris. The whole thing is a little sad. Shaw is sorry for a philanderer because he is sorry for any kind of waste. So Charteris sums up the miserable inanity of his life and the hopeless prospect of his future :

> CHARTERIS. Yes : this is the doom of the philanderer. I shall have to go on philandering now all my life. No domesticity, no fireside, no little ones, nothing at all in Cuthbertson's line.

The two " Unpleasant Plays " that I have dealt with here depict Shaw at once as the fighting dramatist. We travel with him through a forest of thick darkness.   At present we have the problems, with no solutions.   Shaw will not move too quickly.   We must thoroughly understand our problem before we attempt a solution.   That is Shaw's position.   The night is not yet far spent, the hours of darkness are not yet passing away.   We must proceed through the dismal depths of the night before the first glimpse of the embryonic dawn gathers itself hesitatingly to make its later determined onslaught on the powers of darkness.   But Shaw, although in these two plays he merely states the problem, does not allow us to philander.   *Widowers' Houses* has a grave problem ; *The Philanderer* has a lesser problem.   Shaw is beginning very faintly to destroy that he may build up gradually an edifice on a firmer and more permanent foundation.

A SOLDIER AND A CLERGYMAN

HAVING written several " Unpleasant Plays " Bernard Shaw risked all his popularity by writing something that he called pleasant. It was merely a proof of his genius that he did not lose all his public. Shaw had hit at people and they had asked for more. We always like being told we are vicious because we know the criticism applies to our neighbours and not to ourselves. In the " Unpleasant Plays " Shaw was angry with a kind of anger that grips all youngish men when they see that most old men are bored, and many young women are not fools. In the two " Pleasant Plays " that I am writing about in this chapter Shaw is amused, with a certain cynical contempt. Soldiers, well, he doesn't think much of them. And as most soldiers have never heard of Shaw, it doesn't really much matter. Clergymen, Shaw laughs at them a bit, but it does not really matter, as most of them have an ample protection of self-sufficiency.

Arms and the Man is a good play ; *Candida* is a Shavian play. Shaw knows much more about clergymen, effeminate poets and strong-minded women than he does about those curious people who generally join the army to move in the type of society that sees no connection whatever between military culture and the deadly process of war making. Upon

15

the soldier rests all the responsibility of war through-out history : he is the arch criminal and his only real use is when he is dead, and the sooner he is dead the sooner the war comes to an end.

It must be said that in this play concerning soldiers Shaw quite often seems to miss the point. His chief surprise all the way through seems to be occasioned by the fact that a soldier is human, by the fact that even if he wears a red coat it does not cloak his boyishness. The Swiss soldier in *Arms and the Man* is obviously thought about by Shaw as a kind of fancy soldier—the sort of person who might step out of a chocolate box. So far so good. Sergius is a fancy type of soldier. But what Shaw seems to miss is the fact that there is really nothing surprising in soldiers carrying chocolate cream in their pockets, and in nine cases out of ten in war chocolate cream is more useful to a soldier than a Mills' bomb, while the tenth time more frequently than not never happens at all. Shaw makes Raina express a certain amount of polite disgust that Sergius carries chocolate with him into battle. And it does seem that Shaw is also surprised at this, and this merely seems to indicate that he makes the mistake of taking a soldier seriously while pretending to laugh at him. The average soldier in war time has but two ideals—the one is to sleep and the other is to get away on leave as quickly as possible.

I can understand Raina being disappointed that Sergius carries rations of chocolate with him while on active service. What I do not understand is Shaw apparently also being disappointed at this display of an ordinary feeling on the part of Sergius. It looks as though, at the back of his mind, Shaw does really think of soldiers as being perpetually on parade with fixed bayonets and shining buttons. But whether I am right or wrong in assuming that Shaw is disappointed at the humanity of Sergius, it cannot be denied that there is much in *Arms and the Man* that is worth consideration and discussion.

All through the play Raina considers Sergius as a chocolate cream soldier. Now it is probably perfectly untrue that most soldiers are chocolate cream soldiers in the sense of being the kind of military puppets represented on the stage by women who sing patriotic songs to open-mouthed clerks who sit in the gallery and fat business profiteers who slumber in the stalls. But it is true that the average woman is inclined to treat her own particular soldier as though he were a chocolate cream soldier in the sense that he has for her never grown beyond the stage of appreciating chocolate cream.

There is an excellent understanding of the soldier's point of view when Sergius expresses perfectly sincerely his contempt for death, not because death is death, but because death is sleep and the soldier, who has but recently returned from a period of active fighting, does not care for anything but sleep. That it is perfectly possible to march and sleep at the same time is known by every soldier who was foolish enough to fight the Germans in order that England might be delivered into the hands of the profiteer and the feminist. Shaw has got Sergius's desire for sleep perfectly. He has also got perfectly Raina's only gradual understanding of Sergius's sincerity when he

does express his utter contempt for death, since it is
a means of obtaining undisturbed sleep.

> RAINA. Come, don't be disheartened. Oh, you
> are a very poor soldier—a chocolate cream
> soldier! Come, cheer up; it takes less courage to
> climb down than to face capture; remember that.
> MAN. No; capture only means death; and death
> is sleep—oh, sleep, sleep, undisturbed sleep!
> Climbing down the pipe means doing something
> —exerting myself—thinking! Death ten times
> over first.
> RAINA. Are you so sleepy as that?

It is during some casual conversation between the
maidservant Louka and the manservant Nicola that
we discover the position held by Shaw, which may be
a good one or may be a bad one, according to the way
in which we view ambition. Louka remarks with a
certain amount of contempt that Nicola has the soul
of a servant, by which I suppose she means that he
has no particular wish to be anything else than a
subordinate. To this observation Nicola makes the
apt retort that the secret of being a successful servant
is to have the soul of a servant. Now I believe that
Shaw defends this position in so far as it is undoubtedly logical. The man who is content to remain a
clerk will probably do better service as a clerk than
the man who wishes to become a manager. On the
other hand the desire to become a manager may make
a man a more excellent clerk because he knows that
to become a manager he must be a more excellent
clerk than his fellow clerks. This is a particular

example and we cannot, I think, argue dogmatically one way or the other. But there is the general position which, it seems to me, is held by Shaw, and it is expressed here by Nicola. It is that whether ambition is laudable or not, it does breed discontent. The successful servant (or shall I be more correct in saying the happy servant), is the individual who has the soul of a servant, not an inferior soul in any sense at all, but a consciousness that to serve is as much an achievement as being served or being the director of servants. Shaw is right, then, in his assertion that the best servant is the servant in every phase of the word.

It is quite soon after this little discussion on the perfect servant that Shaw tells us something about the imperfect art of the soldier. Sergius explains why he has given up being a soldier, though I strongly suspect he never really was anything more than a man covered by uniform. He sums up in a few words what he considers to be the philosophy of soldiering, and as it is obviously also the military philosophy of Shaw, it is important to see whether there is any truth in it. This, then, is what Sergius says :

SERGIUS. Soldiering, my dear madam, is the coward's art of attacking mercilessly when you are strong and keeping out of harm's way when you are weak. That is the whole secret of successful fighting. Get your enemy at a disadvantage ; and never, on any account, fight him on equal terms.

There is, of course, a certain amount of truth in saying that strategy is very necessary to an army.

The avoidance of battle has won many battles.   The
knowledge of when not to attack is probably more
vital than the knowledge of when to attack.   But it
is an extraordinary thing that Shaw so frequently
manages to be irritating when there is no necessity.
He has explained very reasonably the strategic art of
the soldier but there is no need whatever to have
called it a coward's art.   Soldiering is not the art of a
coward : it is not the art of a brave man : it is the art
of the military artist.   Nothing is probably more necessary to the successful conduct of a battle than common
sense.   He who fights and runs away is not a coward
but a potential Napoleon.   A soldier who can fight in
two battles is more useful than the soldier who
recklessly throws away his life in one.   When Shaw
says that the ideal is not to fight your enemy on
equal terms, he is perfectly right.   A battle between
two armies is in reality a battle of wits.   War, like
commerce, is an unclean business.   The successful
soldier and the successful business man achieve their
success by taking advantage of the weakness of the
other side.   While, then, most of what Shaw makes
Sergius say is true, he makes a mistake in suggesting
military skill to be cowardice.   If there is any
question of cowardice it is not the soldier who is
cowardly but the type of commercial man who
pretends to be friendly while all the time employing
the really cowardly art of pretending to work on
gentlemanly standards.

When Raina observes to Bluntschli that she has
told a lie he retorts with perfect truth that there are
two things which never surprise a soldier.   The one

is hearing lies; the other is having his life saved.
The weakness of *Arms and the Man* is really that the
soldiers in it are too stagey. The retort may be:
What can be expected in a play? The soldiers in a
play must do something. They must climb down
water pipes; they must hide in apple barrels. You
cannot depict on the stage the ordinary life of the
soldier—his absurd life of drilling himself into a
machine so that one day he may have to fight for a
king for whom he has the profoundest contempt.
You cannot depict on the stage the ordinary officer
inspecting chins to see if they are properly shaved.
You must depict him rescued by some foreign lady,
while the enemy pass by on the other side of the
street. But Shaw is not content to have his stage
soldiers and leave them at that. He sets out in this
play every now and again to be really serious, and it is
when he is really serious that he manages to say a
good deal about soldiers which might quite well be
said by a Nonconformist minister who had the ines-
timable privilege of mixing with the local majors at
the local council. I have already criticised Shaw
adversely on the ground that he considers the art of
the soldier to be a coward's art, but I cannot in any
way disagree with him when he says that most soldiers
are afraid of their officers. The average officer, at least
in the British Army, does not treat his men badly and
does not treat them well. He is not really allowed to
do so. The average soldier is afraid of his superior
officer, not in the sense that he fears any violence
from him, but in the way that a school boy feels about
his head-master. There is a great gulf fixed and

neither side can bridge it. That, somehow, is something that Shaw seems to miss. He complains, rather querulously, that the men are afraid of their officers, but does not seem to realise that not only is this a necessary state of affairs but that it is also quite inevitable.

When Shaw makes a kind of half-hearted attack on duelling, he is really amusing. He may well laugh at the rather foolish etiquette which demands that each party in a duel may choose his own weapon. It would then, of course, be quite conceivable that a cavalry officer should choose a sword while an artilleryman chose a howitzer. The ironic conversation between Sergius and Bluntschli on the subject of a duel between them is one of the best parts of *Arms and the Man*. It is an effective attack on the absurd kind of men who, in foreign armies, fly to duels at the least provocation, thereby costing the unfortunate state money while undergoing hospital treatment at the state's expense. The burlesque is an effective attack on the silly kind of militarism which is never content unless it is settling some silly quarrel about some supposed insult. The dialogue is so characteristic of Shaw in an ironic mood that I reproduce it here.

SERGIUS. Captain Bluntschli.

BLUNTSCHLI. Eh?

SERGIUS. You have deceived me. You are my rival. I brook no rivals. At six o'clock I shall be in the drilling-ground on the Klissoura road, alone, on horseback, with my sabre. Do you understand?

BLUNTSCHLI. Oh, thank you; that's a cavalry man's proposal. I'm in the artillery ; and I have the choice of weapons. If I go, I shall take a machine gun. And there shall be no mistake about the cartridges this time.

SERGIUS. Take care, sir. It is not our custom in Bulgaria to allow invitations of that kind to be trifled with.

BLUNTSCHLI. Pooh ! don't talk to me about Bulgaria. You don't know what fighting is. But have it your own way. Bring your sabre along. I'll meet you.

SERGIUS. Well said, Switzer. Shall I lend you my best horse ?

BLUNTSCHLI. No ; damn your horse !—thank you all the same, my dear fellow. I shall fight you on foot. Horseback's too dangerous : I don't want to kill you if I can help it.

Arms and the Man has, of course, many flashes of wit, but it has not the sustained brilliance of some of the other plays of Bernard Shaw. We feel all the time that Shaw does not quite understand military questions, that his brilliance is only a substitute for knowledge by reason of its brilliance. Sergius, the soldier, is a harmless kind of man who fights because he is paid to do so. He has all the time an underlying contempt for his profession which makes him somewhat contemptuous. The women in the play are amusing but not strikingly outstanding. The whole play is something of a joke and yet Shaw is not a spontaneous joker. In pure art and technique *Arms*

c

and the Man is a step backwards from the "Un-pleasant Plays." It is refreshing to be able to leave the spasmodic brilliance of *Arms and the Man* and turn to the sustained excellence of *Candida*—a play which is, in my opinion, one of the best that Shaw has given us.

. . . . . .

In *Candida* Bernard Shaw has done effectively what most playwrights have done ineffectively. He has drawn with extreme skill a stage clergyman and has endowed him with the attributes of reality and common sense. Such a figure is indeed rare. The average stage clergyman is either a thundering blackguard or a pious fool. Morell is not a fool nor a blackguard. He knows the value of his office and he knows even better his own value. He has a working knowledge of mankind and gives God a breezy fraternal friendship. He and God are brothers in arms against the sin of the world and the world is quite tolerably disposed to both of them.

The plot of *Candida* need not detain us long. Marchbanks, a snivelling little poet, in a peculiar sense is in love with Mrs. Morell. Mrs. Morell is flattered by the attention of this poetic little worm, lets him wriggle about in ecstasies of passionate adoration, and then—a little tired of his squirmings—drives him forth, while she returns to her masculine and clerical husband. The plot, as can be seen, is a more or less thin one : the treatment of it is Shaw at a very high level indeed. The admirable way in which Morell manages to exercise a Christian and perfectly un-merited toleration towards Marchbanks is excellently conceived. Morell treats Marchbanks with a toleration which is the highest form of contempt. You can always afford to treat your inferiors in a Christian manner, which is the sole reason why the bishops are kind to the prosperous laymen in their dioceses. Candida herself is a very good example of the type of woman who is flattered by having a lap-dog who has two feet : she is the type of woman who is followed by the sweet type of man whose only mission in life is effectively to prevent the mass òf mankind from becoming sweet.

Let us consider something about this brilliant play. We are plunged straight away into the study of one of those busy clergymen who manage to make the pursuit of God a kind of delirious Grand National. Morell is so broad-minded that he will address any kind of body of thinkers, however contradictory their beliefs or disbeliefs. Such a position is an excellent training for anybody who has to sort out the jig-saw puzzle of contradictions called Christianity. In the study also we find Miss Proserpine Garnett, a quite undistinguished little typist who adores her employer without understanding, which is, after all, a very good reason for adoring one's employer. We see at once how deeply Shaw does understand the fact that a clergyman is always up against the world for the simple reason that what is common sense and commonplace to him seems to be uncommon nonsense to most ordinary mortals. Morell has received an invitation to address a charming set of people who call themselves Communist Anarchists. On looking through the list of vacant dates Miss Garnett finds that there is some difficulty in fitting in the engagement and remarks that, after all, it is not very important as they are only a few ignorant and conceited costermongers without much money. It is then that Morell retorts with that kind of shattering truth which is never quite understood. It is that kind of parsonic ideal which sees through the mass of different types of men some unity postulating a universal Fatherhood. And it is equally true that most clergymen believe in this kind of universal parentage, while most laymen cannot believe it, having been brought up from early childhood to believe that it is their mission in life to destroy any suggestion of a universal brotherhood. If it is true that the average parson believes that we have the same Father in heaven, most of us agree with him while being perfectly happy that most of our brothers have the same Father in hell. Shaw brings out with almost dreadful force the deadly unworldliness of the clerical point of view, which if really acted upon would prove to be of much more economic beneficence to the race than all the financial schemes which are gradually turning the civilised world into a cesspool of commercialism and smoking factories.

PROSERPINE. Guild of St. Matthew on Monday. Independent Labour Party, Greenwich Branch, on Thursday. Monday, Social-Democratic Federation, Mile-End Branch. Thursday, first Confirmation class—Oh, I'd better tell them you can't come. They're only half a dozen ignorant and conceited costermongers without five shillings between them.

MORELL. Ah ; but you see they're near relatives of
mine, Miss Garnett.

PROSERPINE. Relatives of yours !

MORELL. Yes : we have the same father—in
Heaven.

PROSERPINE. Oh, is that all ?

MORELL. Ah, you don't believe it. Everybody
says it : nobody believes it—nobody. Well,
well ! Come, Miss Proserpine ; can't you find a
date for the costers ? What about the 25th ?
that was vacant the day before yesterday.

There is a certain amount of melancholy in the
passage, for nobody does believe what the priest says
about the same Heavenly Father—it would upset our
feeble values much too violently.

Not only does Shaw understand Morell very deeply,
he also understands fully the difference in point of
view of the young curate and the more experienced
vicar. Lexy is quite a pious young man, but he is a
bit too proud of his humility. Lexy is not quite
old enough to put his theories into practice. He will
put the Church first so long as it is not too difficult.
Morell will always put the Church first and never
think about the cost of doing so. This is very well
brought out by Shaw, when Lexy (you cannot blame
the young fellow, life is sweet to him) is a little
doubtful about running the risk of infection that will
be incurred if Candida brings back the children who
have had German measles. Lexy begins quite a
reasonable objection, when it is interrupted by the
unreasonableness of Morell. When the things of God

are at stake you must be, by human standards, un-reasonable.   Such is the type of clergyman created by Shaw.

> LEXY. But, my dear Morell, if what Jimmy and
>   Fluffy had was scarlatina, do you think it wise——--
> MORELL. Scarlatina !—rubbish, German measles. I
>   brought it into the house myself from the Pycroft
>   Street School. A parson is like a doctor, my
>   boy : he must face infection as a soldier must
>   face bullets.

There is the difference. Lexy with all his boyish impetuosity is not really so impetuous as Morell with all his middle-age caution. It is the paradox that is always so startlingly true in life. Shaw knows only too well that the piety of curates is perfectly sincere but a little material ; the joys of Heaven are so far off, they must not be brought nearer. Death, sings the curate in ecstasy, that is the culmination of life, but let this delightful culmination be delayed. Death, says the experienced vicar, come when it may, it will be at the right moment—but, and here is the difference, life in itself is also important.

Again very rightly Shaw has made Lexy something of a prig. Curates are sometimes prigs. For it is unnatural to the young to worry about God. And curates must worry about God when they are not worrying about the effectiveness of their written sermons. Miss Garnett knowing quite well that she is dowdy and shabby is always anxious to impress on other people that she knows their ill-natured thoughts about her. Thus she whines a little pathetically to

Lexy, saying she is quite certain that he thinks her
shabby and cheap and withal of the type of person
who consumes buns and milk in any A.B.C. shop.
Lexy replies with a kind of pious platitude that
is convincingly unconvincing. Shaw quite rightly
makes Lexy unconvincing in his clerical platitudes,
while he makes Morell absolutely convincing.

> LEXY. Heaven forbid that I should think of any
> of God's creatures in such a way!

Once again Shaw brings out so well how the curate
indulging in hero worship tries to follow Morell and
merely succeeds in attaining to a feeble imitation of
him. When Lexy is accused of this he makes a
retort that is perfectly natural. I emphasise this as
there are many Shavian critics who seem to have
completely missed the admirable drawing of Lexy in
their endeavours to write sensibly of the " shindy "
between Morell and Marchbanks concerning the
irritating Candida.

> LEXY. I try to follow his example, not to imitate
> him.

.   .   .   .   .   .

In a quiet way Morell manages to score off everybody he comes in contact with. He scores off his
father-in-law, a self-made business man who over-
dresses his body and under-dresses his manners. Mr.
Burgess is, of course, well conceived by Shaw, but
there is nothing particularly illuminating about his
conception. I mean to say that any front-rank
dramatist could draw Burgess : Shaw, however, can

draw Morell. You will find Burgess in the first-class
compartment of any suburban train, or on any golf
course on Sunday. Morell loses a certain amount
of dignity by deigning to have anything to do with
Burgess at all. It is probably true, as Morell
states, that the wages Burgess pays his women
employées drive them on the streets, but, after all,
a street prostitute is much less pernicious than a
drawing-room prostitute. It is all a little obvious—
the platitudinous clerical attack by Morell on Burgess
for paying low wages. The Church starves its lower
servants and many clergymen might well accuse the
Church of being but a sweating agency.

I must now pass on to the main part of this play.
It is, of course, the absurd infatuation of Marchbanks
for Candida, and the ingenious handling of him by
Morell. Morell never takes Marchbanks quite seriously. Marchbanks never takes himself other than
seriously. Candida is rather amused at the whole
episode. When Marchbanks declares to Morell that
he loves Candida, Morell retorts with a kind of genial
amusement that, after all, most people do like his
wife. The remarkable restraint with which Morell
conducts himself when in contact with the insufferable
little cad that Marchbanks really is, is a proof—if any
were needed—that Morell is indeed a really excellent
follower of the Master for Whom he fights. It is true
that Morell can become a little cross with Marchbanks ; it is a little tiresome to find yourself in
conflict with a beastly little poet who tells you that
you do not understand your own wife, especially as
it would be a dreadful bore if you did. The difficult

part to determine, of course, is whether Marchbanks is really in love with Candida or whether he has merely thought himself into loving her because he is of the opinion that Morell neglects her. I have an idea that we shall hit the truth best if we say that Marchbanks loves Candida partly for her own sake, and partly because he feels that it is his duty to be a kind of " gallant." What most of the critics seem to have missed is that Marchbanks is inordinately conceited. He thinks, not that he can take the place of Morell in any way, but that his championship of Candida will compensate for the alleged indifference of her husband. What, of course, Marchbanks really complains about is that Morell is so public-minded that he has no time to be private-minded. But Marchbanks, as is shown at the end of the play, is all wrong about Candida. She is really bored to death with March-banks. She will allow him to follow her about just because the dear little fool is useful, just because there is no woman born who does not like to be followed about by something or other.

Marchbanks, after a speedy indictment of Morell and his methods, races up to what he considers is a shattering climax. The insolent, little, poetic cad, perfectly safe in taunting a clergyman, asks Morell to look at the Bible. He compares Morell to King David, a comparison which, no doubt, would be pleasing neither to King David nor to Morell. At any rate, it is quite probable—judging by the Goliath story—that King David would have given March-banks a good clip under the jaw, which would have sent him back squeaking to his mother. Be that as it may, Marchbanks suddenly throws at Morell that dreadful sentence which embodies something of the dramatic failure of King David. "But his wife despised him in her heart."

Had Marchbanks searched diligently through the whole Bible, had he even cursed through the cursing Psalms, he could not possibly have found a text which so utterly misinterpreted Candida's opinion of her husband. For Candida looked at her husband, "And behold he was very good." It is when Marchbanks has delivered himself of this most inapt text that Morell gets thoroughly cross with him. Marchbanks counters by behaving like the despicable little hound he is. Shaw has got him to a nicety. Shaw knows full well that he is the type of snivelling little beast who will avoid a good thumping by pretending that he will rid the world of his odious presence. Even Morell, tolerant as he is of Marchbanks, cannot forebear from calling him names, much in the same way that Christ blackguarded the unutterable humbugs who surrounded him in the far-off days in Galilee and who surround Him now, whether it be in St. Peter's, Rome, or the little tin chapel that lies at the top of a gigantic coalmine.

MORELL. Leave my house. Do you hear?
MARCHBANKS. Let me alone. Don't touch me. Stop, Morell ; if you strike me, I'll kill myself ; I won't bear it. Let me go. Take your hand away.
MORELL. You little snivelling, cowardly whelp. Go, before you frighten yourself into a fit.

The attitude of Candida to Marchbanks is well summed up when she tells him almost as if he were an imbecile that if he is a good boy he may help her lay the supper table. What I fail to understand is, how Morell for an instant could even bother to think that Candida could have any unpleasant interest in this horrid little poet.

Very occasionally Marchbanks does express something of the poetic temperament. He does express that feeling which most poets have, whether they be poetic poets or prose poets, that they are in a minority not because of their exceptional talents, but because of their exceptional intimacy with nature. Shaw, as I say, makes Marchbanks a horrid little hound. At the same time, he does make him express not only the sentiments a poet is expected to express, but the sentiments that a poet does express, the sentiments which gain for him unpopularity with the world, which always distrusts anything that cannot readily be turned into money. It is the real and essential reason why the world has always distrusted death. Marchbanks complains a little bitterly that the rôle of the poet is to talk to himself. If only he would. But Marchbanks, in the sentences that I quote here, does express quite admirably that inward communing which, outwardly expressed, resolves itself into that rather commonplace form of expression which we usually label quite fallaciously, as poetry. Miss Garnett, with all the insolence of an unattractive dependant, has told Marchbanks really quite rudely (the poor child should not be spoken to so roughly !) to go and talk to himself.

> MARCHBANKS. That is what all poets do : they
> talk to themselves out loud ; and the world
> overhears them. But it's horribly lonely not to
> talk to someone else sometimes.

Poor Morell, if he can appreciate all kinds of queer
people, he cannot appreciate poets. Or is it Marchbanks ?

He has no sympathy with the romantic fancies of
Marchbanks. He has no patience with the idea that
you may make a scrubbing brush into a sailing boat.
Shaw is very consistent in his delineation of Morell.
He is intensely, boringly practical. He would be
quite surprised if you told him his creed was a great
romance and that to walk on water is no less a
poetic fancy than flying to fairyland on a scrubbing
brush.

So Marchbanks muses sadly and the muses will
give him but scant comfort. For Candida is out of
his reach.

> MARCHBANKS. No, not a scrubbing brush, but a
> boat—a tiny shallop to sail away in, far from
> the world, where the marble floors are washed by
> the rain and dried by the sun ; where the south
> wind dusts the beautiful and purple carpets. Or
> a chariot ! to carry us up into the sky, where the
> lamps are stars, and don't need to be filled with
> paraffin oil every day.

To which Morell rejoins with quite unnecessary
harshness.

Morell. And where there is nothing to do but to be idle, selfish and useless.

It would almost seem as if Morell had seen in imagination the orthodox picture of Heaven!

.   .   .   .   .   .

The contempt which Morell feels for Marchbanks rises to its climax when he trusts his wife alone with the young poet. Nothing could be more uncomplimentary to him. Shaw has made his clergyman treat his " enemy " in the most contemptuous way possible, by suggesting that the poet is harmless to Candida. What a blow to the conceited little person. But the poet does not see through the contempt. It is a little later that we find how utterly bored Candida is with Marchbanks—she cannot even listen to his poetry! It would be impossible to find any more hopeless love affair than that between Marchbanks and Candida. But it is not a love affair, it is all one sided. Shaw certainly understands both Marchbanks and Candida—Candida certainly does not understand Marchbanks. There is a delicious piece of dialogue when the poet reads and Candida is quite uninterested.

Candida. But you are not boring me, I assure you. Please go on. Do, Eugene.

Marchbanks. I finished the poem about the angel a quarter of an hour ago. I've read you several things since.

And so we come to the inevitable bitter end of this fine play. Candida only cares for her husband; she is not really even particularly sorry for having allowed Marchbanks to make a fool of himself. It is at the end of the play that Shaw gives us some of his finest writing. Marchbanks, a young old man, goes out into the cruel cold world that will treat his poetic fancies with that cynical contempt that it gives to all poets unless they be of sufficient genius to make the world see the odious trend of its ways. Poor Marchbanks is as old as the world. Let him go, the poor little lap dog, and let Candida go back to her clerical husband and let her be received by all his pious parishioners as the nice wife of our good parson. And let Marchbanks talk to the daffodils, they will listen better to his poetry than the pitiable wife of Morell.

CANDIDA. Will you, for my sake, make a little poem out of the two sentences I am going to say to you? And will you promise to repeat it to yourself whenever you think of me.

MARCHBANKS. Say the sentences.

CANDIDA. When I am thirty, she will be forty-five. When I am sixty, she will be seventy-five.

MARCHBANKS. In a hundred years, we shall be the same age. But I have a better secret than that in my heart. Let me go now. The night outside grows impatient.

And soon, Morell and Candida, the night will grow impatient for you to be gone, but you will not be able to follow the poet. For it is only very young children and very young angels who can follow poets.

The "Pleasant Plays" of which I have chosen two are Shaw in a mood of satire. Whatever we may think of the plays and their morals it is foolish to deny that in Morell Shaw has drawn one of the most convincing clergymen seen on the stage for some time. Morell is a man and a priest. Shaw never misses the combination. He has drawn Morell with deep sincerity. When all is said and done *Candida* is a sad play. For it is always sad to see a young man make a fool of himself over a woman and it is especially melancholy when the woman is most decidedly not worth the trouble. Candida is not worth while bothering about. She is just an ordinary wife, made extraordinary by the false vision of a silly young poet. The best we can say for Marchbanks is that while he whines quite often, when the inevitable does come he does not whine. Morell, Marchbanks, Candida are three of the best of the Shavian characters. They are so admirably blended that the worst in all of them is brought out with great skill. And the best in all of them falls naturally into place. Shaw, the careful artist, has painted with great care. *Candida* is a fine picture perfectly harmonised.

Chapter III

TWO LITTLE WAR PLAYS

IN part of his preface to *Heartbreak House* Bernard Shaw explains why he did not write more plays with a definitely anti-war bias. He says something which is quite unpleasantly true. He says that while war is on you cannot employ the theatre to make war on war. This is, of course, obvious. It is no use for the theatre to endeavour to preach sanity when the nation has gone mad. It is merely waste of time for the theatre to employ the talent of its playwrights when every two-penny-halfpenny citizen is a shilling-a-day soldier. And there is, as Bernard Shaw points out, a more difficult and deeper reason. While a war is in process it is inconvenient for the public to know the truth and, it might be said in passing, it is just as inconvenient for the public to know the truth in peace time. Otherwise the spectacle of every nation secretly preparing for war would be a little disquieting all round. In war time the theatre must make people laugh. It must provide comedy in the theatre of make-believe while tragedy is played twice nightly in the theatre of war. The soldier returning from the trenches has to be amused by a bevy of vulgar chorus girls who prepare him quite admirably for a subsequent period of folly with a street woman who is, after all, in some ways contributing to the

general health of the army and is certainly not so
evil as the detestable clergy who preach war in the
pulpit.

Bernard Shaw, then, being good enough to contribute something to the theatre's output during the
Great War, wrote two quite admirable little war
burlesques which had more than a smattering of truth
in them.   The war did not affect the genius of Bernard
Shaw adversely : the two little war plays that I
discuss here though small in quantity are not small in
quality.   They deal on the one hand with the curious
position brought about by the enforcing of a warlike
régime in a country like England and on the other
with what a fêted soldier really thinks about it all.

I will consider first of all the delightful little satire,
Augustus Does his Bit.   It would hardly be possible
to have found any more reprehensible word than the
word " bit " which was given equally to war service
done by soldiers at the front and to the war service
done by those who sheltered in England.   From the
soldier's point of view, his bit usually meant that
either he was blown to bits or that his job at home
was stolen by some woman who was doing her bit,
and, incidentally, doing the soldier out of his bit.
Augustus is typical of the kind of person produced by
the war.   He is the worst kind of patriot : he is the
man who loves his country so much that he is always
willing to let other people die for it.   He is the type
of Englishman who would be quite incapable of
earning his living if he did not happen to have it
earned already for him.   He is the type of Englishman
who speaks like a gentleman and, though he does not

D

know it, behaves like a cad.   He is a zealous follower
of the local fox hounds and can be seen any winter
morning in company with the cultured male and
female savages who represent English aristocracy and
English hypocrisy.   Dear Augustus, when the play
opens, is doing his bit in an English country town
which, for the time being, has turned its usual
lethargic inhabitants into a number of war-made
enthusiasts.   The God of the parish church has armed
Himself with a bayonet: the daughters of the
Vicarage attend the Holy Communion on Sunday and
help to fill high explosive shells on Monday.   Most of
the able-bodied men of the town have gone to the
Front and all the sons of the county houses have
become quite holy and spotless, for " dear Gerald "
and " darling Harry " have become Second Lieu-
tenants.

When the play opens Lord Augustus Highcastle is
very much annoyed to find that one old clerk represents all the members of his staff.   The clerk, who
has been to volunteer and has been rejected, is
extraordinarily truly drawn.   Bernard Shaw knows
well enough that the only thing that worried the
rejected volunteer was his quite frequent inability to
get his railway fare to the recruiting station paid.
The average soldier did not care a brass farthing for
his country ; he cared a little less for the King and
considerably less for God.   So we find the clerk
grumbling that he has not had his fare paid.   But if
there is one person who does know what the average
soldier feels about the humbugs who surround him,
it is Bernard Shaw.

CLERK. They said they wouldn't have me if I was given away with a pound of tea. Told me to go home and not be an old silly. Young Bill Knight, that I took with me, got two and sevenpence. I got nothing. Is it justice? This country is going to the dogs, if you ask me.

How little the enthusiastic nobleman realises the inconvenience of a universal patriotism which sends everybody to the front, is well brought out, when the clerk explains with some insolence and no little humour that he is the secretary as well.

THE CLERK. I'm the Secretary. I can't leave the room and send myself to you at the same time, can I?

This little war play, although it is amusing, is also serious enough. Shaw deals cleverly with the fact that recruiting speeches which piled on the agony did not have much tangible result. Many would-be soldiers on hearing that thousands of soldiers were dying at the front remained " would-be " soldiers.

When then Lord Augustus complains that he made his best recruiting speech and no one joined, the result is what might quite well be expected. So many of those in a high position will not face the fact that many people have no ideals whatever. Many of the working class do not want to fight for their country. Why should they? Their whole life is one long, weary fight to keep body and soul together. They are not deluded by the promises made by those who have always lived in the lap of luxury. They are not in

the least troubled if Germany wins or not, so long as
their meagre salary, their trivial amusements, are not
interfered with.   Poor Augustus is dreadfully disappointed at the poor results of his eloquence.

> AUGUSTUS. This town wants waking up.   I made
> the best recruiting speech I ever made in my
> life ; and not a man joined.

To which complaint the clerk replies with a great
deal of truth.   It is disappointing to know that many
Englishmen have no wish whatever to fight for England but it is better to realise this than to go about
proclaiming the patriotism of the English and then
have to explain away the necessity of a very rigid
conscription.

> THE CLERK. What did you expect ? You told them
> our gallant fellows is falling at the rate of a
> thousand a day in the big push.   Dying for Little
> Pifflington, you says.   Come and take their
> places, you says.   That ain't the way to recruit.

Augustus jumps to rather a silly conclusion.   Shaw
has drawn him quite truly.   The men won't fight
because they are afraid.   Could there be anything
more untrue ? The Englishman is not afraid to fight
but he objects to fighting people for no reason at all.
There has never been one valid reason why any
soldier should have fought the Germans.   He had no
quarrel with them, the only reason that made him
fight was discipline.   The hatred of the Germans was
to be found in the ranks of those who stayed at home,
the bombastic curates, the pitiable bishops, the

horrible women who waved to the departing troops.
As the clerk explains—let the Germans come to Little
Pifflington and the inhabitants will fight soon enough,
but why should they hate men in the German trenches,
whose existence they never even knew of.

> THE CLERK. They got grudges again' one another :
> how can they have grudges again' the Huns that
> they never saw ? They've no imagination : that's
> what it is. Bring the Huns here ; and they'll
> quarrel with them fast enough.

I am not sure whether Shaw is at all correct in
assuming that the non-desire to fight implies want of
imagination. I am inclined to think that it was the
possession of a ready imagination which prevented
many men from becoming soldiers. What really
frightened them was not going to the front, but the
coming back to this country to find their jobs gone,
their wives (many of them) unfaithful, this land in
the hands of profiteers and prigs.

In all his arguments with Augustus the Clerk really
gets the best of it. He represents the point of view of
the ordinary man who has a far stronger hold on truth
than is usually imagined. Augustus mentions with a
great show of bombast the fact that everybody during
the war is making selfless sacrifices. Unfortunately
the reverse is the case. The majority of people in
England took the opportunity of making a good thing
out of the war. If it be asked what they did in the
Great War it might be answered with obstinate
vulgarity that they did everybody they could. Shaw
holds Augustus up to ridicule, but we ought to realise

that in a feeble sort of way Augustus meant to do well. England had no more dangerous kind of enemy. So when, without thinking deeply on the question, Augustus comments glibly on the way people are sacrificing themselves for the war, the Clerk (being much more in touch with the common people) knows only too well that the converse is the case. Shaw does show us here that the commonplace man did probe a good deal deeper than the higher officials. It was obvious that they could not, because they had to express an enthusiasm and patriotism that conscription proved was conspicuous by its absence. The dialogue that I reproduce here is really delightful and is the ironical Shaw at his best.

> AUGUSTUS. Our gallant fellows are dying in the trenches ; and you want a rise !
>
> THE CLERK. What are they dying for ? To keep me alive, ain't it ? Well, what's the good of that if I'm dead of hunger—by the time they come back?
>
> AUGUSTUS. Everybody else is making sacrifices without a thought of self ; and you——
>
> THE CLERK. Not half, they ain't. Where's the baker's sacrifice ? Where's the coal merchant's ? Where's the butcher's ? Charging me double : that's how they sacrifice themselves. Well, I want to sacrifice myself that way too. Just double next Saturday : double and not a penny less ; or no secretary for you.

The play develops into pure, rich humour when Augustus is not too busy to see a lady who combines high rank with good looks. The way in which he

makes himself out to be, even in this interview, merely
a gallant patriot, depicts his self-sufficiency excellently. Shaw, with unerring skill, deals with one of
the side curses of the war—the disgusting petticoat
influence, against which only a very few of our big
men were able to stand. Augustus is not man enough
to resist a beautiful woman. The two people who
appeared to be able to do this in the war have not yet
been discovered ! Once again the dialogue is the kind
of dialogue that no one but Shaw can write. It has
that mixture of humour, truth and contempt which
distinguishes so much of his work. There is a half
sneer behind the laugh—the laugh just prevents the
sneer from being totally unpleasant. Augustus cannot conceal his eagerness to see the handsome young
female—the national peril must wait until he has
finished seeing her.

> AUGUSTUS. Stop. Does she seem to be a person of
>   consequence ?
> THE CLERK. A regular marchioness, if you ask me.
> AUGUSTUS. Hm ! Beautiful, did you say ?
> THE CLERK. A human chrysanthemum, sir, believe
>   me.
> AUGUSTUS. It will be extremely inconvenient for
>   me to see her ; but the country is in danger ; and
>   we must not consider our own comfort. Think
>   how our gallant fellows are suffering in the
>   trenches ! Shew her up. Stop whistling in-
>   stantly, sir. This is not a casino.
> THE CLERK. Ain't it ? You just wait till you see her.

Towards the end of the play, the plot of which is

simply that an attractive woman gets some papers
out of Augustus for a wager, Augustus makes one of
those cynical remarks which do not seem quite to fit
in with his mentality. It can only be supposed that
Shaw had changed places with him. He makes a
cynical and slightly futile remark about the House of
Commons, that house which proves that a party
of politicians can get quite a lot done. Augustus
suggests that, during a war, no one takes any notice
of the House of Commons. It would be a much truer
observation which said that there would be probably
no war if we took no notice of the House of Commons
at all. The House of Commons made the war with
Germany and it has entirely failed ever since to make
the peace.

> AUGUSTUS. The great advantage of being at war,
> madam, is that nobody takes the slightest notice
> of the House of Commons. No doubt it is some-
> times necessary for a Minister to soothe the more
> seditious members of that assembly by giving a
> pledge or two ; but the War Office takes no
> notice of such things.

It is when the Clerk has become a soldier that
Shaw manages to say something which is rather
foolish. He suggests, out of the mouth of Augustus
is he condemned, that as the Clerk is now a soldier he
can expect no more fair treatment. Such a position
is about as absurd as any position Shaw has ever
taken up. There is no class of justice so fair as
military justice : no civil court can compare favour-
ably with a court martial. If Shaw had remarked

that a man could expect no fairness from an ecclesiastical court he might have been right. All through
history the civil courts have administered justice with
a moderation of efficiency : all through history
ecclesiastical courts have administered justice with
the kind of spirit that Christ most hated : all through
history the military courts have administered justice.

THE CLERK. I'll have the law on you for this, I
will.
AUGUSTUS. There's no more law for you, you
scoundrel. You're a soldier now. Thank
heaven, the war has given us the upper hand of
these fellows at last. Excuse my violence ; but
discipline is absolutely necessary in dealing with
the lower middle classes.

Augustus Does his Bit expresses what many people
felt during the war—that patriotism was much more
popular with those who had a good material share of
England than with those whose only claim to English
soil was six foot in the churchyard. Augustus
thrived during the war : he thrives to-day. The
Clerk existed during the war : to-day he does not
live, he just exists in the country which has awarded
his services with a contemptuous indifference. Leaving
England for a moment we find ourselves in Ireland
in company with O'Flaherty who is typically Irish in
the sense of being a typical diplomat.

· · · · · ·

The preface that Bernard Shaw wrote to his
common-sense little play *O'Flaherty, V.C.*, comprises a

really quite excellent consideration of the question of
the Irish soldier in the British Army. The Irish
soldier is different from the British soldier in the
sense that he is more spectacular and probably less
reliable. It is perfectly true, as Bernard Shaw says,
that the average British officer, while disliking the
Irish soldier, likes to have some of them in his bat-
talion. The reasons for this apparent contradiction
are, according to Shaw, two. The one, that an
Irishman values his life less than an Englishman, the
probable reason being that he reads the New Testament with more intelligence ; the other that the most
inefficient Irishman in matters of courage wants to
outdo the English soldier. What is the truth in these
two assertions ? Seriously, there is probably not
much truth in either of them. The Irishman is
not careless of his life : why should he be, when
the average Irish soldier knows full well that his
friends and relations have not sufficient money to
get him a decent remission out of Purgatory. The
Irish Protestant soldier, like the English Protestant
soldier, are both equally afraid in war. The average
Irish soldier, as I have seen him, was not in the
smallest degree interested in outdoing the English
soldier. As long as his rations came up to the front
line, as long as he was relieved at the proper period,
as long as he got his six days' leave, he cared for
little else. It is, perhaps, true to say that the English
soldier rather liked to outdo the ill-mannered Colonial
soldiers, but he certainly felt no rivalry in the Scotch
or Irish regiments. If Bernard Shaw had sometimes
carried a rifle in his hands instead of a pen, it would

have saved him from writing a good deal that is untrue.

However, a little later in the same preface when Bernard Shaw deals with the question of British political policy and the question of Irish recruiting, we find that everything he says is devastatingly true. The British Government during the war excelled itself in its abominable treatment of Ireland. With a degree of superficiality which is positively astonishing, the British Government asked Ireland to remember Belgium. What, of course, the British Government should have done if they wanted to induce Irish recruiting on an enthusiastic scale, would have been to chalk up in the largest possible letters " Forget England," or, as Bernard Shaw says with exquisite truth, " Forget and forgive."

And it is again unfortunately perfectly true that the British Government did, quite unnecessarily, reduce Dublin to something of the horrid mess to which the Germans (who had some conceivable right for doing so) reduced Louvain and Rheims. As Bernard Shaw points out, the British Government really indulged in quite a jolly little joke.

" On the smouldering ruins of Dublin the appeals to remember Louvain were presently supplemented by a fresh appeal. Irishmen : do you wish to have the horrors of war brought to your own hearth and home ? Dublin laughed sourly."

Bernard Shaw gives a very good reason why the Irish joined the colours. It is a reason that is not by any means a monopoly of the Irish.

" No one will ever know how many men joined
the Army in 1914 and 1915 to escape from tyrants
and task-masters, termagents and shrews, none of
whom are any the less irksome when they happen
by ill-luck to be also our fathers, our mothers and
our children."

He does not add, as he well might, in how many
homes in England, Ireland, Scotland and Wales there
was much fervency of prayer that the gallant soldier
who had left for the front might find an honourable
grave in a foreign country while his wife at home
found a new and less honourable bed-partner.

Let us turn to a consideration of O'Flaherty, V.C.,
and let us not forget, as we consider the gallant
soldier, that it is still a very long way to Tipperary
and a great deal farther than it would have been to
Berlin.

O'Flaherty is the type of soldier who sees through
the type of people who make a fuss of him.   The
soldiers who returned from the Front were not hood-
winked by the cheers of London nor the plaudits of
local mayors.   They were not gratified to find that
the women who waved pocket handkerchiefs at them
had also waived them the right to their own jobs.

O'Flaherty, V.C., is being entertained by General
Sir Pearce Madigan, an elderly baronet who is quite
a good fellow as are most baronets, their baronetcy
contributing slightly to their goodness.   Bernard
Shaw, with keen psychology, makes us sense at once
that the gallant V.C. is enjoying himself with that
kind of exquisite agony which always comes when the

subordinate is entertained by his superior officer or
his employer. A ball in the servants' hall is held for
the servants. In the same way well-meaning people
who visit the workhouse on Christmas Day sometimes
add to the embarrassment of the inmates. It is
all so inevitable. With the best will in the world
you cannot escape class consciousness. General
Sir Pearce Madigan is absolutely sincerely anxious
that O'Flaherty shall have a pleasant day. But
O'Flaherty must rise when his superior officer enters.
You cannot make him quite at ease.

> Sir Pearce. No, no, O'Flaherty; none of that
> now. You're off duty. Remember that though
> I am a general of forty years' service, that little
> cross of yours gives you a higher rank in the roll
> of glory than I can pretend to.
> O'Flaherty. I'm thankful to you, Sir Pearce; but
> I wouldn't have anyone think that the baronet
> of my native place would let a common soldier
> like me sit down in his presence without leave.
> Sir Pearce. Well, you're not a common soldier,
> O'Flaherty; you're a very uncommon one; and
> I'm proud to have you for my guest here to-day.

But Sir Pearce Madigan soon finds that the V.C.
is not quite so easy to entertain as he had supposed.
Shaw brings out very well the supreme difference in
point of view of a man who has a position of wealth
in a country and a peasant who really does find it
difficult to live at all. However much we may feel
that patriotism should not be dependent upon possession, the fact does remain that the rich are usually

more patriotic than the poor. And I do not mean
here the poor who are merely well-bred people with
little money, nor do I refer to the rich who are ill-bred
people with plenty of money. Thus the General puts
his point of view concerning love of King and love of
Country, and O'Flaherty puts his. And it is not
merely the rather disloyal Irishman speaking, but the
possessionless man who makes up two thirds of the
population of any country in the world. O'Flaherty
has complained that he is a little tired of all the fuss
that is being made about him, especially as he knows
that he does not really deserve any of it. Thus does
Shaw by means of clever dialogue depict the inevitable
clash between the General and the private soldier—
two people who are quite nice and pleasant in their
own totally opposite ways.

> SIR PEARCE. Yes, yes ; I know. *I* know. One
> does get fed up with it : I've been dog tired
> myself on parade many a time. But still, you
> know, there's a gratifying side to it, too. After
> all, he is our king ; and it's our own country,
> isn't it ?
> O'FLAHERTY. Well, sir, to you that have an estate
> in it, it would feel like your country. But the
> divil a perch of it ever I owned. And as to the
> king, God help him, my mother would have taken
> the skin off my back if I'd ever let on to have any
> other king than Parnell.

It is also extremely well brought out by Shaw here
how exceedingly untrustworthy are not only Irish-
women of the peasant class but all women of the

lower classes. I have little doubt but that it would be a sincere shock to the good people of many an English village to know that the dear old lady who greets the lord of the manor at the lodge gates with a fervent, " God bless you, Sir," means in reality, " God blast you, Sir."

Mrs. O'Flaherty's pretended loyalty has quite taken in the poor old General.

> SIR PEARCE. Your mother ! What are you dreaming about, O'Flaherty ? A most loyal woman. Always most loyal. Whenever there is an illness in the Royal Family, she asks me every time we meet about the health of the patient as anxiously as if it were yourself, her only son.

Although the play descends at times to pure farce, it is never entirely farcical. The wonderful stories that O'Flaherty invents to obtain recruits are, of course, exaggerated, but the recruiting posters were not above showing the potential recruit an imaginative version of the blessings of being a private soldier. But even enthusiastic as Sir Pearce Madigan is for the bringing in of devotees to the colours, he admits that O'Flaherty's description of how he fought the Kaiser single-handed is a little likely to be questioned as to its strict authenticity. So with keen knowledge of character Shaw makes the General remonstrate with O'Flaherty.

> SIR PEARCE. Well, in recruiting a man gets carried away. I stretch it a bit occasionally myself. After all, it's for king and country. But if you

won't mind my saying it, O'Flaherty, I think
that story about your fighting the Kaiser and
the twelve giants of the Prussian guard single-
handed would be the better for a little toning
down. I don't ask you to drop it, you know ;
for it's popular, undoubtedly ; but still, the
truth is the truth. Don't you think it would
fetch in almost as many recruits if you reduced
the number of guardsmen to six ?

The essence of the play is reached when O'Flaherty
quite suddenly breaks into a somewhat violent
denunciation of patriotism. It is, I suppose, what
many of the Irish feel—that England is a kind of
enemy who has ever kept Ireland poor and down at
heel. I give O'Flaherty's outburst, lengthy as it is,
because it does show with some force what the vassal
does feel about certain things when he has got rid of
his inherent subserviency to the ruling classes and
says outwardly what he has said inwardly ever since
he could say anything at all.

O'FLAHERTY. It means different to me than what
    it would to you, sir. It means England and
    England's king to you. To me and the like of
    me it means talking about the English just the
    way the English papers talk about the Boshes.
    And what good has it ever done here in Ireland ?
    It's kept me ignorant because it filled up my
    mother's mind, and she thought it ought to fill
    up mine too. It's kept Ireland poor, because
    instead of trying to better ourselves we thought
    we was the fine fellows of patriots when we were

speaking evil of Englishmen that was as poor as
ourselves and maybe as good as ourselves.   The
Boshes I kilt was more knowledgable men than
me ; and what better am I now that I've kilt
them ? What better is anybody ?

At the end of the play Sir Pearce Madigan asks a
question which Shaw has already asked, and I think
most people would agree that the answer O'Flaherty
gives is the answer that most of those who want to
see in war service a fine gesture of self-sacrifice are
careful to forget.

> SIR PEARCE. Strictly between ourselves, O'Fla-
> herty, and as one soldier to another, do you think
> we should have got an army without conscription
> if domestic life had been as happy as people say
> it is ?
> O'FLAHERTY. Well, between you and me and the
> wall, Sir Pearce, I think the less we say about
> that until the war's over, the better.

The two little war plays depict quite vividly much
of Bernard Shaw's attitude towards our wicked war
with Germany and towards war in general.   He does
not mince matters.   War, he feels, drives out the
small amount of intelligence that we happen to have.
Incidentally, it seems to have driven some out of
Bernard Shaw. The technique of the plays seems to
me to be extraordinarily good.   They race to a finish
and end just when they should end.   The characters
appear to me to be truly drawn and much more truly
drawn than are the military characters in *Arms and*

E

the Man. The war produced a considerable mass of mediocre literature and moderate poetry, and in the theatre a number of war plays that were quite good as long as the war lasted. We are now thinking about peace and consolidating our thinking about it with a mass of war literature which is educating the young in qualities the exact opposite from those which the peace fanatics imagine. We are so enamoured of peace, our logic is so invincible, that the Host carried through the streets is guarded by armed soldiers. And it is left to me to point out this amazing anomaly. Be that as it may, we may do quite a lot in the way of promoting peace by occasionally reading the war plays of Bernard Shaw and by occasionally telling any chance young officer we may happen to meet what an amazing person he really is.

CHAPTER IV

A PLAY FOR PURITANS

*T*HE *Devil's Disciple* is a play that wavers between being political and being theological. It might, indeed, be mistaken for a religious play. Religion and politics being the two subjects upon which most people quarrel, Shaw has always been interested enough to leap into the fight. *The Devil's Disciple* is a play for Puritans in the sense that it is a play for those who object to the austerity, not to say ungeniality, of the Puritans. The whole play is in the nature of a paradox. The Devil's disciple is really a good friend of God. Mrs. Dudgeon, like some Christians, is a quite admirable ally of Satan. The plot of the play is a simple one and can be dismissed in a sentence or two. It is merely a melodrama of the Saturday night Lyceum type which concerns the wrong man who is nearly hanged, the right woman who manages nearly to behave sensibly, a parson who is too much of a gentleman to believe what he teaches. As usual, it is not the play that is important, but the playwright. The essence of Shaw's position is that Dick Dudgeon is really so religious that he is driven from his Puritanical home by the religious people in it. Mrs. Dudgeon combines with great facility the art of the religious expressor with a capacity of never making the error of following the spirit of religion. Mrs. Dudgeon is entirely true to herself : she grasps religious platitudes as she would grasp money : she spurns sin as she would spurn charity : she is appalled at the wickedness of her son, and never looks in the looking-glass.

Richard Dudgeon is one of those pleasant people who cannot help being profane. He blasphemes the God he likes intensely : he has a contempt for his mother of the reciprocal kind which demonstrates itself in explosions of abuse, for Dudgeon is too clever to waste subtlety on Mrs. Dudgeon. Anderson, the Puritan chaplain, is quite an excellent example of the type of clergyman who has an exasperating habit of frequently saying the right thing. Nothing is more fatal to a clergyman. It is the will of God, pipes the pious curate, entering the death chamber of one who is choked to death with cancer. We cannot blame the curate ; if he said what he really thought he would be merely one more individual to be added to the quota of unemployed issued weekly by the Minister of Labour. Without the platitudes of our clergy we should all go mad. For it is one of the chief functions of the Church to prevent us from taking things as they appear to be.

Anderson always manages to behave as a gentleman, and he has the somewhat unusual merit of behaving in a gentlemanly manner to his wife. Such a position is not so usual as may be thought. Mrs. Anderson, not a particularly striking type of character, hates Richard Dudgeon with that feminine hatred which is nearly always an unrecognised form of affection. Mrs. Anderson is in love with her husband in the way that most wives are in love with their husbands, in the way that they are a useful piece of furniture without which the rooms would look strangely empty. She does not, perhaps, trouble very greatly about him while he is there, but she shows a much truer form of affection by worrying when he is not present. It is one of the most unfortunate of commonplaces and one of the truest of truisms that we cannot appreciate what we have. We cannot appreciate the person out of the coffin as much as the person in it.

There are two problems which arise somewhat forcibly in any discussion on this admirable Shavian play and I shall reserve any investigation of them until the end of this chapter. Meanwhile, I wish to consider in some small detail some of the situations and arguments that occur during the course of the play.

. . . . . .

It is fairly early in the first act that one of the quite minor characters in *The Devil's Disciple* says something that the Puritans really did believe. The Puritans undoubtedly did believe in that kind of equality which is always being expressed and is never really expected to be taken literally. After all, quite a number of us are of the opinion that we are equal in the sight of God, but we are most of us particularly careful to emphasise how unequal we are in the sight of man. *The Devil's Disciple* is an excellent play for showing the care that Bernard Shaw displays on his minor characters. It is this trait that makes him such a fine dramatist. The minor characters are quite as important as brilliant dialogue, for after all, a play is a picture of life, and life would be quite unlivable without the minor characters in it. Shaw has never suffered from laziness ; he is not the type of dramatist who thinks that because some of his characters say little he can quite easily let that little mean nothing. Thus when Essie, being somewhat effectually bullied by the unpleasant Dudgeon relations, promises to fall in line with what they want, Shaw makes Uncle William not only reply to her as he certainly would reply, but adds a kind of platitude which is a very efficient interpretation of Uncle William.

> UNCLE WILLIAM. That's right ; that's right. We know who you are ; but we are willing to be kind to you if you are a good girl and deserve it. We are all equal before the Throne.

The last sentence in this quotation emphasises the unerring genius of Shaw for depicting the natural psychology of a character rather than (as is so often the case in the theatre to-day) the playwright's psychology of the character.

It would have been comparatively easy for Shaw to have exaggerated Dick Dudgeon by letting him be too rude to the people he meets. He is not exactly over-rude to the chaplain—he just treats him as something which is quite hypocritical. He is sorry for Mr. Anderson ; he is sorry for the man who has to throw sermons before swine. It is the fate of many clergymen and it is unfortunate that the clergy, although mystically endowed with the spirit of Christ, have not His power of driving the swine down to the sea.

On the other hand, Richard is certainly extremely rude to the chaplain's wife. He insults her abominably by telling her that she looks good. It is an insult, for most women who look good are too dull to be anything else. But it is very important, I think, to realise that Dick Dudgeon hates Mrs. Anderson because she makes him feel that in some ways his rakishness is rather silly.

It is towards the end of the first act that Dick explains why he is on the side of the Devil. It is most important to notice what he says for it is in a limited sense Shaw taking the unpopular side. Dudgeon takes the side of the Devil because he is such an extremely good Christian. Dudgeon takes the side of the Devil because he demands that the world cringes before the Conqueror of the Devil, not because it loves the Conqueror, but because the world is frightened of the Devil's Conqueror. This is, of course, to say that we are religious merely through fear of the consequences. I think Shaw would be nearer the mark if he had said that many of us were religious because it was a material advantage to be so. The grocer who preaches atheism in the market-place and underpays his errand boy needs no errand boy for long. The grocer who is a sidesman of the local church and underpays his errand boy soon has to employ two. However, here is Dick's unfaltering confession and, if it is quite good for his own soul, it is equally good for the soulless people whom he slates.

RICHARD. Because it's true. I was brought up in the other service ; but I knew from the first that the Devil was my natural master and captain and friend. I saw that he was in the right, and that the world cringed to his Conqueror only through fear. I prayed secretly to him ; and he comforted me, and saved me from having my spirit broken in this house of children's tears. I promised him my soul and swore an oath I would stand up for him in this world and stand by him in the next. That promise and that oath made a man of me. From this day this house is his home ; and no child shall cry in it : this hearth is his altar ; and no soul shall ever cower over it in the dark evenings and be afraid. Now which of you good men will take this child and rescue her from the house of the Devil ?

It is in the second act that we soon discover Anderson to be a great deal more sincere than Dudgeon would have us believe. He really is quite contemptuous of his own life with that contempt that is a part of the man who has a proper perspective. He remarks that there is always danger for those who are afraid of it. There is, of course, much more danger for those who are not. But it is a different kind of danger. Anderson can brave the dangers of earth because he can brave the dangers of Heaven. He depicts in no small measure how very much more rational the average man is than the average woman, or rather it might be fairer to say that Anderson gets the essence of a situation very much more quickly than does his wife. For instance, Mrs. Anderson is really quite sincerely worried about her feelings of hatred

for Dudgeon.   She knows it is wrong to hate people :
she does not in the least realise that it is not by any
means a near approach to the worst evil.

Anderson corrects her admirably when he says only
too truly that the grave sin is not hatred but indifference.   Shaw brings this position out with tremendous
force—with something of the force with which Mr.
Belloc brought it out when he argued that Death, far
from being the worst evil, was a minor evil compared
with the loss of human affection.   Now this is obviously true.   If we are indifferent to people we are
no longer human because we have turned traitor to
our natural instincts, and they must atrophy through
neglect.   But if we hate, we have not played traitor
to our instincts : we have merely deflected them and
have every chance of bringing them back to that
straight but narrow gate which is the difficult portal
of the entrance to Heaven.   Anderson then encour-
ages his wife that, after all, she is not in such a bad
way even if she does hate.

> ANDERSON. Come, dear, you're not so wicked as
> you think.   The worst sin towards our fellow
> creatures is not to hate them, but to be indifferent
> to them :   that's the essence of inhumanity.
> After all, my dear, if you watch people carefully,
> you'll be surprised to find how like hate is to love.

If Anderson is quicker at seeing the essence of a
situation than his wife, the chaplain is also better at
argument than Dudgeon.   Shaw has shown with
almost cunning the fact that Dudgeon does believe
that abuse is a form of argument.   He does not seem

to see that it is not only no form of argument but is
undoubtedly bad form.   The whole matter really is,
I think, that in many ways Anderson is cleverer than
Dudgeon and Shaw is cleverer than either of them.
When Anderson invites Dudgeon to tea, he retorts to
the invitation with the superficiality that Anderson is
merely civil to him because he has succeeded to his
father's estate.   Now it is perfectly obvious that
Anderson is never the type of man to be pleasant to
another man because he may gain by it.   Nor is he
the type of man to refrain from being pleasant to
another man because he may not gain by it.   Anderson invites Dudgeon to tea because he believes in
turning the other cheek and because he does believe
(and so few of us unfortunately do) that violence can
be conquered by gentleness, that the disciple of the
Devil can be persuaded, not by bribes but by a picture
of that sincerity which is not a cloak, as Dudgeon
believes, for hypocrisy.   The few lines that I quote
here do bring out very vitally the attitude of Anderson
to Richard and the attitude of Richard to Anderson,
and also the fact that Anderson, with his gentleness
towards life, has made a much more violent onslaught
on it than Dudgeon with his not theatrical but
desperado violence.

RICHARD. Raining like the very —— I beg your
    pardon ; but you see —— !

ANDERSON. Take it off, sir ; and let it hang before
    the fire a while ; my wife will excuse your shirt-
    sleeves.   Judith ! put in another spoonful of tea
    for Mr. Dudgeon.

RICHARD. The magic of property, Pastor! Are
even you civil to me now that I have succeeded
to my father's estate?

ANDERSON. I think, sir, that since you accept my
hospitality, you cannot have so bad an opinion
of it. Sit down.

A little later on we find that if Anderson gets the
better of an argument with Dudgeon, Dudgeon is
more vital in argument than Mrs. Anderson. Mrs.
Anderson remarks with all the pride of possession that in
any case she would rather be married to her husband
whom everybody respects than to Dick Dudgeon who
is far too sincere to gain the respect of anybody.
Richard brings out very easily that, while Anderson
might conceivably put him on the right road, Mrs.
Anderson might quite easily put him on the wrong
road by being so evilly good. Richard is, of course,
having tea with Mrs. Anderson as Anderson has gone
out to minister to Mrs. Dudgeon who, in spite of being
quite heartless, has had an extreme heart attack.
Dudgeon, almost caught off his guard, envies the
placid home of Mrs. Anderson, as the wanderer does
envy such a dwelling place, at the same time knowing
full well that, even if he had the chance of such a
haven of rest, he would soon wander out again.

RICHARD. I am thinking. It is all so strange to
me. I can see the beauty and peace of this
home; I think I have never been more at rest in
my life than at this moment; and yet I know
quite well that I could never live here. It's not

in my nature, I suppose, to be domesticated.
But it's very beautiful; it's almost holy.

JUDITH. Why do you laugh?

RICHARD. I was thinking that if any stranger came
in here now, he would take us for man and wife.

JUDITH. You mean, I suppose, that you are more
my age than he is.

RICHARD. I never thought of such a thing. I see
there is another side to domestic joy.

JUDITH. I would rather have a husband whom
everybody respects than—than——

RICHARD. Than the Devil's disciple. You are
right; but I daresay your love helps him to be
a good man, just as your hate helps me to be a
bad one.

The third act of *The Devil's Disciple* is particularly
interesting as depicting Bernard Shaw (it is his
seventy-third birthday as I write these words) dealing
with melodrama. We find that Shaw practises with
keen ingenuity the difficult art of restraint. It is not
easy to write an enthusiastic play: it is less easy to
write a restrained one. Shaw has hit the happy
medium. He is both enthusiastic and restrained.
Dick Dudgeon has changed places with the chaplain.
Such a situation might be handled quite excellently
by any ordinary playwright. Bernard Shaw not only
handles the situation but lets the situation handle a
good deal of his philosophy. The central part of this
act is, of course, the indictment of the chaplains who
do their worst at an execution.

During the scene when the chaplain is ministering

to Dudgeon we have some very effective retorts to his
pious efforts.   The chaplain, with all that superficiality which distinguishes the official clergyman, is
naturally a little incensed at Dudgeon's refusal to take
any notice of what he says.   With a good deal of
insight Richard remarks that an execution is no place
for a chaplain.   Bernard Shaw is perfectly right.
We have no right whatever to send a man violently
out of the world knowing full well that the chaplain
who ministers to him is merely a government-paid
official and merely part of the legal machinery which
carries out the law.   The chaplain at an execution
merely demonstrates the appalling failure of Christianity.   If Christian ministers did their work properly
there would be no need for executions.

So Richard tells the chaplain that he isn't wanted.

RICHARD. Look here, sir ; this is no place for a
    man of your profession. Hadn't you better go
    away ?

In reply to this piece of insolence the chaplain
remarks, probably believing what he says, that
Richard must submit to the Divine Will.   Richard
replies in the words that I reproduce herewith.   They
are, I think, at least one point of view and do suggest
quite strongly that feeling that many people have
that executions are quite an unchristian method of
punishment and are merely a return to the background
of an era which demanded that God was a kind of
greedy monarch desiring a tooth for a tooth, an eye
for an eye.   I think it is quite obvious that Shaw
would agree with the sentiments that Dudgeon here

expresses and I do not fall into the error of supposing that Shaw is always speaking for himself through his characters. But he usually is when there is any kind of problem as hinted at here.

> RICHARD. Answer for your own will, sir, and those of your accomplices here ; I see little divinity about them or you. You talk to me of Christianity when you are in the act of hanging your enemies. Was there ever such blasphemous nonsense ! You've got up the solemnity of the occasion as you call it, to impress the people with your own dignity—Handel's music and a clergyman to make murder look like piety ! Do you suppose I am going to help you ? You've asked me to choose the rope because you don't know your own trade well enough to shoot me properly. Well, hang away and have done with it.

We then find that the chaplain is quite determined to do his best. No doubt Shaw intends us to be angry at the insistence of the chaplain which seems to be almost bad form. At the same time we must be fair. The chaplain has to be the interpreter of a creed which demands that one effort to convert is by no means enough, that the lost sheep must be sought in the hedges, in the byeways, and even, I suspect, on the scaffold. But to take the play as it is. Shaw does make Dudgeon retort in a way that makes a fine dramatic situation and also does express with subtlety the popular dislike of mixing up religion with the exigencies of the law. The whole fact of the matter is that both the chaplain and Dudgeon can find a good deal to support their opposing points of view.

We are perhaps inclined to miss this, Dudgeon in his position of extremity naturally inciting our sympathy and thereby possibly impairing our judgment.

SWINDON. Can you do nothing with him, Mr. Brudenell?

CHAPLAIN. I will try, sir. Man that is born of woman hath——

RICHARD. " Thou shalt not kill."

Probably the real objection to a chaplain being present at an execution is not so much the incongruity of his presence as the fact that he adds to the mental anguish of the prisoner. Shaw certainly seems to imply this for he makes General Burgoyne get to the root of the matter when he remarks with some show of surprise that Dudgeon is in a hurry to be hanged. Life is no doubt sweet but death is sweeter when the hangman's rope can be seen. If we are to be hanged let it be done quickly. Let us be free from fuss, a good stout rope is all we need. There will be plenty of time to apologise to God when we have got to the other side. Dudgeon merely asks that the whole beastly business be got on with at once. His remonstrance is most effective and might be considered by those who are not appalled at a condemned criminal having to attend service in the prison chapel.

RICHARD. Do you think this is a pleasant sort of thing to be kept waiting for? You've made up your mind to commit murder : well, do it and have done with it.

The Devil's Disciple is a consideration of values. Bernard Shaw sees our religion is so dreadfully topsy-turvy. The religious people are hard and disagreeable (probably because religion is a desperate fight), the irreligious people are just religious. Anderson gets tired of his official ministrations ; Dudgeon gets tired of his rather peevish bargain with the Devil, simply brought about by the nasty bigotry of his mother. Just before the end of the play Anderson sums up the whole position very reasonably.

ANDERSON. Sir ! it is in the hour of trial that a man finds his true profession. This foolish young man boasted himself the Devil's disciple ; but when the hour of trial came to him, he found that it was his destiny to suffer and be faithful to the death. I thought myself a decent minister of the gospel of peace ; but when the hour of trial came to me, I found that it was my destiny to be a man of action and that my place was amid the thunder of the captains and the shouting. So I am starting life at fifty as Captain Anthony Anderson of the Springtown militia ; and the Devil's disciple here will start presently as the Reverend Richard Dudgeon and wag his pow in my old pulpit and give good advice to this silly, sentimental, little wife of mine.

Shaw cannot resist a jolly little joke though there is a deep truth behind. It is that we were not meant

to hang people, that the judge's natural instinct is to
ask a man to lunch rather than to assume the black
cap. It is our awful muddle of everything that has
made us sometimes kill a man when we would really
rather that he ate a plate of ham and beef with us.
So Burgoyne asks Dudgeon to lunch, having just
avoided hanging him.   As I say, the joke is a serious
Shavian joke.

BURGOYNE. Oh, by the way, Mr. Dudgeon, I shall
be glad to see you at lunch at half-past one.

. . . . . .

I have now to discuss the two problems I mentioned
earlier in this chapter. They are firstly—why Dick
Dudgeon allowed himself to be nearly hanged in the
place of Anderson and secondly—whether it is not an
exaggeration to draw Mrs. Anderson as falling in
love with Dudgeon, when she had hated him quite
intensely.
In considering the character of Dudgeon we can
certainly be assured that he is quite a fearless character. He obviously was not the type of man to tell the
court-martial it had made a mistake so that he might
save his own skin. He most undoubtedly did not
wish to save Anderson because he liked him or even
because (quite grudgingly) he respected him.   He
did not, I think, keep silence about the mistake
because he wished to save Mrs. Anderson the misery
of having her husband executed.   Such an explanation
would make Dick more of an ordinary character than
he is.   There is surely only one explanation and it is

F

that explanation that is never quite explainable. Dick was willing to suffer in the place of Anderson just because it happened to come his way to do this thing.   Shaw gives us the reason why Dick was willing to save Anderson.   It is that humanity is a fine thing at bedrock, that the first instinct is to die for someone else (hence perhaps the reason why the Crucifixion is the central part of Christianity, a thing Shaw has always failed to see) that instinct that sends a man into the sea to rescue a stranger, that instinct which makes a porter jump in front of an express train to save the life of someone he may not even see well enough to know by sight.   What Shaw complains about is that the critics who asked why on earth Dudgeon should have saved Anderson will not even trouble to read the daily press where they may see every day " how some policeman or fireman or nurse-maid has received a medal, or the compliments of a magistrate or perhaps a public funeral, for risking his or her life to save another's."

Yes, that is the answer to our first problem.   And it is perhaps the answer to Pilate's desperate question —that truth is only that which never seems quite obvious to anybody because it is almost too true to be seen.   Dudgeon's conduct is not too good to be true, it is too good to be false.   We only think about saving our own life when there is no one else's life to be saved.   Dick was not a hero, he was not even brave, he was just a man who could not help himself being born with the imprint of the Man who saved the world on Calvary because the job came His way.

*   *   *   *   *

In dealing with the problem as to whether Mrs.
Anderson would have reversed her hatred of Dudgeon
and turned it into love, this is not quite so easy of
solution as might be thought. We may say that love
is akin to hate and think we have solved the problem.
We have not, for I cannot see that Mrs. Anderson
might have had her feelings of hate for Dick changed
to feelings of love just because he was so willing to
sacrifice himself for her husband. I am sure (even
though all women upset all accepted standards) that
Mrs. Anderson would have outgrown her hate and
given to Dick an outpouring of respect which might
have developed into mere liking. The only explanation
that I can see is that in reality (she would be quite
unconscious of it) Judith Anderson loved Dick all the
time. This is a very commonplace attempt to solve
the problem, no doubt, but it seems to me much
more reasonable than to suppose that Judith suddenly
changed because Dick was to die a violent death.

The only other explanation I have is not an explanation at all. It is an apology. And I feel that in this
instance Shaw did not carry out a development to its
logical conclusion, that he jumped at a conclusion and
failed to bring off a convincing climax. I feel, then,
that either Shaw created an untrue *dénouement* or
that we have to read between the lines and discover
that all the time Mrs. Anderson loved Dick. I must
confess I am ill satisfied with that suggestion and I
am less ill satisfied with the one which suggests that
Shaw was human enough to create a popular situation
at the expense of accuracy.

The Devil's Disciple is a very obvious play that had

the reception it might have expected. The critics failed to see that Dick was never in love with Judith, they failed to see that Dick's action in going to the gallows was not heroic, it was just that indefinable instinct which makes brothers of us all.

Shaw warns us not to make our religion too hard and not to think that a violent austerity is necessarily true. In a word he seems to imply that Puritanism was not at all pure, that if it stripped religion of beauty, it did very often strip God from the Cross and set up in His place the Devil.

And many men looking up at the Cross and seeing the Devil hanging there would give their allegiance to him, not because they believed in him, but because they could not believe in the Christians who had torn Christ down from the Cross and set up other crosses on which to crucify Him again and again. Shaw has given us a paradoxical play with a dualism, that the man who is willing to lose his life finds it, that the man who loses God has never lost Him at all.

PART II

A MEDICAL DILEMMA

MAN, SUPERMAN, AND A WOMAN

SHAW AND MARRIAGE

CHAPTER I

A MEDICAL DILEMMA

THE main difficulty in dealing with Bernard Shaw's consideration of the medical profession is now and again that it is written by a man who is brilliant in words and less brilliant in thought. *The Doctor's Dilemma* is, of course, merely considered as a play, full of the usual scintillating dialogue that characterises Shaw's work in the theatre. But that is not sufficient. The play is a very serious discussion about the profession of the doctor. Quite simply Shaw makes out that most doctors are hypocritical humbugs, who not only make mistakes but glory in them. Before discussing this play it will be as well to look at a few points raised by Bernard Shaw in his preface on doctors. It is, of course, a preface on Bernard Shaw and is a picture of that deplorable generalising which sometimes destroys the uncanny sanity which is the real and essential Shaw.

Shaw starts straight away with a very silly complaint that the medical profession is, in reality, a murderous one because it has to cut people up. He has made an attempt to cut up doctors but the instruments he uses are abominably blunt. What he seems to imagine is that because you pay a Harley Street surgeon fifty guineas or a hundred guineas to cut off your leg, you are inducing a trend of opinion which will make a large number of expert scientific men consider it desirable to take to leg-cutting as a means of making money. Shaw says that it is quite absurd " to give a surgeon pecuniary interest in cutting off your leg." Obviously it would be a very disgraceful state of affairs if eminent surgeons cut off legs to make money, but it is a vastly different thing if they make money by cutting off legs. The reason a surgeon gets a big fee for his leg-cutting is the simple fact that he is an expert at his job. The reason Bernard Shaw gets big royalties for quite often indulging in the " unscrupulous " game of pulling the leg of the public is that he is an expert dramatist.

Having railed at something Shaw calls the infamous character of the medical profession, he tells us with a show of surprise that it is a remarkable thing that there is a king or queen left alive in Europe to-day, because the doctor who removes a royal personage's blue blood corn receives an advertisement which makes him famous for life. It would have been interesting if Shaw had been able to look forward some years when he wrote this preface and could have seen the King of England put together and made whole almost as a jigsaw puzzle is put together.

Shaw deals at some length with the question of operations. Now it is, of course, a popular objection and it is not by any means confined to that type of mind which denies the reality of material disease, that, quite bluntly, medical men are much too fond of the use of the operating knife. Let us leave this objection on one side for the moment. Shaw goes a good deal further. He suggests that the patient who is operated upon induces in those who are sick a feeling of envy. The sick patient, so Shaw asserts, sees the person who is operated upon the centre of a number of sympathetic gestures. He is the hero of the moment, he is the centre of attraction. For the moment it is of supreme importance whether he lives or dies. All the skill of the doctors and nurses is used on his behalf. For the moment he is like the leading man— all eyes are fixed on him. Thus, Shaw argues that a number of people who have a very sincere wish to be, even at considerable risk to themselves, in the limelight, desire, probably almost involuntarily, to be operated upon. In this way, then, does Bernard Shaw put his argument.

" There are men and women whom the operating table seems to fascinate; half-alive people who through vanity, or hypochondria, or a craving to be the constant objects of anxious attention or what not, lose such feeble sense as they ever had of the value of their own organs and limbs. They seem to care as little for mutilation as lobsters or lizards, which at least have the excuse that they grow new claws and new tails if they lose the old ones."

There is, surely, very little sound reasoning in this objection. Every doctor knows that he has a considerable number of neurotic patients, but there are few, if any, who would allow themselves to be operated on just for the sake of being the objects of a public pity. Nor do I believe that most surgeons use the knife as the first resort.

Another question that Bernard Shaw goes into is

the one that complains that many doctors are kept rich by chronic patients who need constant but commonplace attention and provide a definite income for the practitioner who attends them. This is, of course, true, but does not in any way prove doctors to be unscrupulous. These patients, quite naturally, do provide money for the doctor. Suppose, for a moment, it be conceded that patients are kept alive to put money into the pocket of the doctor, there would be a vastly greater outcry were it proved that the doctor refused to attend a rich patient on moral grounds.

There is, of course, a very long discussion on the question of vivisection, and Bernard Shaw has really nothing new to say. But I cannot pass over an excellent attack that Shaw makes on the loathsome and vile specimens of human nature who fox-hunt and kill animals because they are too cowardly to end their own miserable lives. So Shaw describes his violent disgust at finding himself on the platform at a large anti-vivisection meeting with " blood-sport " devils and vile women who wear hats and cloaks ornamented by the trapping of animals. But Bernard Shaw need not worry too much. The day of our "sportsmen " and "sportswomen " is a waning day and the everlasting damnation of their souls is only a matter of time. Bernard Shaw's attack on various forms of tolerated cruelty (tolerated because we are afraid of offending our friends) must be reproduced here, for the whole attack is about as true as his attack on doctors is false. Why Shaw, who hates cruelty, should attack doctors, who are by nature the kindest of men, is a

matter of surprise. So Shaw describes the people he
found on the platform with him at the Queen's Hall.
It proves what we have always felt, that although
Shaw does unfortunately attack very unfairly at
times, he has always been a man of supreme courage,
standing out in a generation that is too easily tolerant
of cruelties.

> " The ladies among us wore hats and cloaks and
> head-dresses obtained by wholesale massacres, ruth-
> less trappings, callous extermination of our fellow
> creatures. We insisted on our butchers supplying
> us with white veal, and were large and constant
> consumers of *paté de foie gras* ; both comestibles
> being obtained by revolting methods. We sent
> our sons to public schools where indecent flogging
> is a recognised method of taming the young human
> animal. Yet we were all in hysterics of indignation
> at the cruelties of the vivisectors. These, if any
> were present, must have smiled sardonically at such
> inhuman humanitarians, whose daily habits and
> fashionable amusements cause more suffering in
> England in a week than all the vivisectors of Europe
> do in a year."

To sum up, the main objection that Shaw has, not
to doctors individually but to the medical profession,
is that the doctor derives financial benefit from his
attendance on the sick. From this, he argues that,
to put it quite baldly, the doctor finds disease a paying
proposition. So he does. But what Shaw seems to
fail to realise is that every doctor deals with a great
deal of disease which pays him nothing, or, perhaps

less often, pays him by giving him the disease he is endeavouring to cure. Bernard Shaw's position is, in my opinion, superficial, and although his preface on doctors is thought-provoking, it is also provokingly free from any real thought. Much of it, I repeat, is absurd and refuses to take note of the real philosophy of healing. Shaw deals with the outward shell and he makes the supreme mistake of taking things to be as they look. Shall we not understand the medical profession best if we admit that the work of the doctor makes money, but that the doctor does not work to make money.

Let us turn to a consideration of *The Doctor's Dilemma*—a play which brought Shaw a great deal of hostility, most of which, I am bound to say, I think was deserved. The doctors in the play are not by any means rogues, but they are worse. They are foolish, and Bernard Shaw is obviously more foolish in expecting them to be all-wise. The plot is an extraordinarily simple one and need only be stated very briefly. The problem is whether medical skill should be employed to try and cure a brilliant artistic genius who is stricken with consumption, and has also all his life been stricken with moral consumption. I am not sure, really, that in real life the problem would ever arise at all. A doctor would not dream of considering whether he was saving the life of a deplorable scamp : he would be dealing with a case and would give the best of his skill in the hope of making a successful cure. However, Bernard Shaw does discuss this problem as to whether such a scamp as Louis Dubedat is worth saving because, though he

is a scamp, he is also an artist of considerable genius.
So much, then, for the problem.   Now for a discussion
of various situations in the play.

·   ·   ·   ·   ·   ·

In the first act of *The Doctor's Dilemma* Shaw is
much concerned with the unreality of progress.   He
seems to be of the opinion that all progress (at least
in the medical world) tends to move backwards.   He
contends that many of our discoveries merely take us
back to the same positions that our grandfathers
rejected.   Ridgeon, while not exactly laughing at an
alleged new discovery, shows that it is only new to a
new generation.   The dialogue is here natural enough
and Shaw is trying to show us that behind the doctor's
mind there is always a certain feeling of scepticism.

> RIDGEON. You keep up your interest in science, do
> you?
> SIR PATRICK. LORD! yes. Modern science is a
> wonderful thing.   Look at your great discovery!
> Look at all the great discoveries !   Where are
> they leading to ?   Why, right back to my poor
> dear old father's ideas and discoveries.   He's
> been dead now over forty years.   Oh, it's very
> interesting.

Sir Patrick is very careful to point out that we must
beware of setting too great a store on what may
be called the scientific " new " position which may
but prove to be an old untenable position abandoned.
So the eminent doctor puts the thing (as it seems to
Shaw) in the right perspective.

SIR PATRICK. Don't misunderstand me, my boy.
I'm not belittling your discovery.   Most discoveries are made regularly every fifteen years ;
and it's fully a hundred and fifty since yours was
made last.   That's something to be proud of.
But your discovery's not new.   It's only inoculation.   My father practised inoculation until it
was made criminal in eighteen-forty.   That broke
the poor old man's heart.   Golly ! he died of it.
And now it turns out that my father was right
after all.   You've brought us back to inoculation.

Which perhaps merely proves that a prophet has
no honour in his own generation.

Shaw is quite obviously sceptical about the use of
experiments.   They are a dilemma.   The patient may
die under the experiment and he may die without it.
What is he to do ? Live naturally and die naturally
when the time comes.   The whole point that Shaw
seems to have against such an experiment as inoculation is that its curative qualities are so uncertain that
there is not indicated any necessarily good or bad
result from the application of the test.   It is a matter
of luck, some patients get well, some get better.   Or
is it that some have reached the proper time for death
and some have not ? Sir Patrick has found the
dilemma too much for him and so he has given up
modern inoculations.

SIR PATRICK. I could have told you that.   I've
tried these modern inoculations a bit myself.
I've killed people with them ; and I've cured

people with them ; but I gave them up because
. I never could tell which I was going to do.

I have not space to go into all the delightful
arguments that take place between the various doctors
in this play.   The conclusion that Shaw comes to is
that all specialists have a pet theory and that the
disease must be made to fit the theory.   One of the
most amusing bits of typically Shavian dialogue
occurs when there is a debate about germs.   Poor
little germs.   If they do not exist, they ought in
common decency to do so.   They ought to support
the medical profession, but I am afraid quite often
they let it down badly ! Sir Ralph Bloomfield Boning-
ton, who literally " oozes " prosperity, remarks quite
casually that a certain germ must be found and killed.

SIR PATRICK. Suppose there's no germ ?
B.B. Impossible, Sir Patrick ; there must be a
    germ ; else how could the patient be ill ?
SIR PATRICK. Can you show me the germ of over-
    work ?
B.B. No ; but why ? Why ? Because, my dear
    Sir Patrick, though the germ is there, it's in-
    visible.   Nature has given it no danger signal for
    us.

Blenkinsop, the doctor who is too poor to be able
to digest his own poor food, is excellently drawn. He
is typical of the professional man who just manages
to keep soul and body together without detriment to
the former.   He argues with really desperate logic
that his difficulty is to know how to prescribe for his

patients when most of them are much too poor to be able to turn the prescriptions into medicine. Once more—Shaw's favourite theme—the curse of poverty, that poverty which makes a man shoot his wife rather than that he should see her slowly starve to death while the rich man's wife promenades along the " Promenade des Anglais " and regains the health she has lost through overworking at idleness.

As poor Blenkinsop says only too truly: " They daren't be ill, they cannot afford it."

In the creation of Louis Dubedat, Shaw is very happy indeed. Shaw is never so happy as when he is drawing a person who is charming enough to be a crook. Dubedat has all that plausibility which never takes in people when they have become dehumanised. Louis will make a fine art of borrowing money and will make a still finer art of never paying it back. He can draw an exquisite picture and he himself is the most exquisite picture in his wife's eyes. Mrs. Dubedat, like most women, does not see that her husband is a scamp, for love is not only blind but paralyses all the mental faculties. Dubedat is deliciously pleasant, it is almost a pleasure to be cheated by him. He has a quite excellent habit of receiving advance fees for a picture and then forgetting to finish the picture. He finds the pack of doctors a most excellent pack of hounds who, for a long time utterly fail to discover the scent of a fox in their midst. The doctors are so overwhelmed by the chance of having a grapple with tuberculosis that they fail to see that Dubedat is consumed with laughter at their childlike credulity. Only let a man possess some kind of outstanding

genius and his moral qualities do not matter until
they are found out. Then commonplace humanity
having preached at length that genius excuses any
conduct, reacts with the horrid cry that " only the
pure in heart can see God," which, of course, means
that God does not even know genius by sight.

But the medical admiration for genius soon evapor-
ates when the doctors discover that Dubedat has the
greatest possible objection to leaving any of them
untried for money. I feel that Shaw is driving home
the lesson that, unfortunately, people are so seldom
what they seem to be that even men of science do not
probe very deeply when confronted by that most
charming of all the flowers in the garden—the man
with an easy manner. It must not, I think, be forgotten that Shaw is also commenting on the fact that
no profession is free from the influence of women.
The doctors are first interested in Dubedat not because
he is an artistic genius or crammed to the brim with
consumption, but because his wife is the type of wife
who is fortunately always married to someone else.
Louis adores his wife, as do all men when they can
behave like blackguards without their wives finding
out. Such is the height of matrimonial bliss. Dubedat
is always on a pedestal, although as an artist his
proper place is to be below the pedestal. Mrs.
Dubedat is really a sweet woman : she is courageous
enough to tell her husband that he is to come to her for
money whenever he wants it, and Louis is far too
much of an artist to refuse to do so. Poor Louis is
becoming seriously embarrassed by the fact that most
of his commissions have now to be delivered before he

G

gets any money.   He naturally complains that people
care for nothing but money. Mrs. Dubedat pets Louis
with all that affection which is bestowed on a man
who is full of genius and full of germs.

In Act III of *The Doctor's Dilemma* we find that
Louis expresses something of that contempt for
medical men which is shared by Shaw.   Louis is
quite certain that the only reason that the doctors
want to consult about his case is that they will find
the curing of a rising artist a good advertisement.
Dubedat is an extremely practical person : he tells
the eminent specialist who is to sound his lungs that
it would be much more useful if he wrote him out a
cheque instead of messing about with a stethoscope.
As we get to know more of Dubedat we discover that
he is really little more than a crook :   with a little
training he might quite easily become a cad.   He is
not content with borrowing money from the doctors
—he must needs steal a cigarette case which has been
lent him by one of them.   Whether we are to infer
that Dubedat has lost all sense of morality through
his disease, or whether we are to infer that he is a
natural thief, is not easy to determine.   I fancy that
Shaw would believe Dubedat to be the type of thief
who would forget to return things that were lent to
him.   It is a much safer form of thieving : it is easier
to prevent a man from replacing a cigarette case in
his pocket than to take it out.   The lines of dialogue when Walpole wants his cigarette case back
indicate delightfully that Dubedat, however short
he may be of money, has always an excuse up his
sleeve.

WALPOLE. By the way, I'll trouble you for my cigarette case, if you don't mind.

LOUIS. What cigarette case?

WALPOLE. The gold one I lent you at the Star and Garter.

LOUIS. Was that yours?

WALPOLE. Yes.

LOUIS. I'm awfully sorry, old chap. I wondered whose it was. I'm sorry to say this is all that's left of it.

WALPOLE. A pawn ticket!

LOUIS. It's quite safe : he can't sell it for a year, you know. I say, my dear Walpole, I *am* sorry.

At the end of Act II, Sir Patrick, with a kind of burst of enthusiasm (which so seldom distinguishes the professional man because he is afraid it may extinguish him) comments on the undoubted fact that however worthless the medical profession may be as a healer of bodies, it is undoubtedly useful as being an ever-present picture of the spirit that does attempt to mend something. Sir Patrick seems here to look upon the medical profession not as a kind of antiseptic to the poison of modern life but as a provider of the soul-satisfying matter which the arts so lamentably fail to provide. He seems to say, in effect, " we are tired of good books, we are more tired of bad pictures, we are deafened by the discordant noises of the jazz bands : let us find solace and comfort from the rich smell of deadly drugs and medicines that float through the key-hole of the sickroom and denote the highest of all art—the attempt to make whole that which is sick in body and sick in soul."

Sir Patrick does put very clearly that feeling of usefulness which all doctors feel, even when their arms grow tired with writing death certificates.

> SIR PATRICK. Colly! when you live in an age that runs to pictures and statues and plays and brass bands because its men and women are not good enough to comfort its poor aching soul, you should thank Providence that you belong to a profession which is a high and great profession because its business is to heal and mend men and women.

.   .   .   .   .

In *The Doctor's Dilemma*, in Act IV, Bernard Shaw gives us quite a considerable insight into that emotional part of his mind which has been so very much displaced by his more general cold, hard dialectic. Shaw is usually a little too angry to be emotional : he has developed too keenly his sense of sociological attack to allow himself, except now and then, to give full rein to his power of writing that kind of writing which is full of the rather hackneyed human appeal. I refer to the very fine piece of writing that describes the death of Louis Dubedat. Oscar Wilde when dying in a third-rate hotel in Paris (perhaps to punish the first-class hotels who had mocked him in his dishonour) remarked that he was dying beyond his means. Louis Dubedat not only dies beyond his means, he dies considerably beyond his rather objectionable meanness.

To the end of his life Louis is an artist : his wife never gets the right picture of him ; he confuses her with the colours he can mix together. The actual

scene when Dubedat dies with the doctors all around
and the newspaper reporter waiting to get a good story
out of the death of a prominent artist is conceived by
Shaw with a considerable amount of delicacy. I
think the introduction of the newspaper man is a
mistake on his part, but as he was largely made by
the press, he is merely conforming to a popular human
weakness of attacking his helpers. I reproduce here
part of the scene when Dubedat dies, as it indicates
the power Shaw has of describing the intense moments
of life when humanity is real and the only time that
most humanity is real is when it is gathered round
the bed of someone who is sensible enough to die
without being inartistic about it.

> MRS. DUBEDAT. Yes, dear. Sleep. Sh-sh! please
> don't disturb him. What did you say, dear?
> I can't listen without moving him.
>
> WALPOLE. He wants to know is the newspaper man
> here.
>
> THE NEWSPAPER MAN. Yes, Mr. Dubedat. Here I
> am.
>
> MRS. DUBEDAT. Oh, that's right, dear; don't spare
> me; lean with all your weight on me. Now you
> are really resting.
>
> SIR PATRICK. Let me put him back on the pillow,
> ma'am. He will be better so.
>
> MRS. DUBEDAT. Oh, no, please, *please*, doctor. He
> is not tiring me; and he will be so hurt when he
> wakes if he finds I have put him away.
>
> SIR PATRICK. He will never wake again.
>
> MRS. DUBEDAT. Was that death?
>
> WALPOLE. Yes.

Immediately after this really superb piece of writing and understanding of character, Shaw makes one of those extraordinary drops to a kind of cheap banality. Let us remember that Louis Dubedat has only just died; we are to imagine that his eyes are wide open and see nothing; his jaw has dropped and there is that kind of shocked silence which always succeeds the tension of the passing of a human being. Now Walpole has proved himself in the play to be a rather one-idea man. Every disease is to him a case of blood poisoning. But I cannot see any indication at all that he was the type of man to make a caddish remark about a person lying in front of him but very newly dead. The remark that Shaw puts into Walpole's mouth is, I am certain, an instance of a very gross misunderstanding of character. It is quite remarkable how Shaw can recede from first-class drama to the kind of dramatic art which entirely forgets that it should depict logical human beings. The doctors remark that if, after all, Dubedat was a scamp and a rotter, he did do the one thing that is of supreme importance to the Englishman—he did die decently, and Walpole's remark which I quote here seems to be out of place altogether.

> B.B. My dear Colly! The poor lad! He died
>   splendidly.
> Sir Patrick. Aye! that is how the wicked die.
>   For there are no bands in their death;
>   But their strength is firm;
>   They are not in trouble as other men.
>   No matter: it's not for us to judge. He's in
> another world now.

WALPOLE. Borrowing his first five-pound note there, probably.

RIDGEON. I said the other day that the most tragic thing in the world is a sick doctor. I was wrong. The most tragic thing in the world is a man of genius who is not also a man of honour.

I am certain that Walpole would not have made this beastly remark. I am also equally certain that Shaw has made a very great mistake in letting the newspaper man talk in this way:

THE NEWSPAPER MAN. Do you think she would give me a few words on "How It Feels to be a Widow"? Rather a good title for an article, isn't it?

The reply to this brazen piece of offensiveness is no doubt true to life. But why should Shaw insult journalists in this way? Simply because he loses control of himself when writing of people he thinks to be mere idiots.

B.B. Young man: if you wait until Mrs. Dubedat comes back, you will be able to write an article on "How It Feels to be Turned Out of the House."

At the end of Act IV there is rather a surprising kind of speech by Mrs. Dubedat. It is that in some rather mystical way Louis has caused by his death an emotion that is at once universal and beautiful. In a word, Dubedat has died artistically, and Mrs. Dubedat will ever go through life with the remembrance of having shared it with a beautiful artist.

Life can never be sordid for her because Louis has shown that it is beautiful in essence. It is true that she did not know his very many failings, but even if she had, I feel that Shaw would have us believe that there was some kind of exquisite germ of living which evolved into some more exquisite germ of dying. She expresses, as so many of us do not express well, that the death of Dubedat has been an experience, and subsequent experiences will always be coloured by it. She is all the time so utterly unaware that there was anything about her husband that was worthless. She is the type of woman who can ever see the artist but can never see the man. That is why, perhaps, all true artists are surrounded by women who are attracted by their careless unconventionalism which expresses itself in meaningless caresses and, perhaps unconsciously, uses woman as the inspiration that produces beautiful pictures. It is most important, I think, that we should realise that we should accept that Mrs. Dubedat, although she would never admit it, does not ever discover her real husband. And I think it is also obvious that Louis did love her well enough not ever to let her do so. Thus Mrs. Dubedat seems, to me, to sum up her real approach to life and her rather unreal approach to her husband.

MRS. DUBEDAT. I felt that I must shake hands with his friends once more before we part to-day. We have shared together a great privilege and a great happiness. I don't think we can ever think of ourselves as ordinary people again. We have had a wonderful experience ; and that gives us

a common faith, a common ideal, that nobody
else can quite have.   Life will always be beautiful
to us : death will always be beautiful to us.
May we shake hands on that ?

.   .   .   .   .

Once more just before the end of the play Mrs.
Dubedat expresses about her husband something that
I am sure many people feel but do not have the
courage to express, that art is in itself so noble that
the artist must never consider the more popular art
of self-sacrifice, if it is to frustrate the brilliance of
his art.

JENNIFER. He was one of the men who know what
women know : that self-sacrifice is vain and
cowardly.

And I think that Shaw is right when he suggests
rather hopelessly that the world as a whole does not
appreciate artists who are bad men, but it appreciates
still less good men who are bad artists.   But then the
world never appreciates any combination of excellence.   It rejected Christ because it was utterly
dazzled and blinded by a Person who was a perfect
Man and perfect Artist.   Christ died as only a perfect
artist could—utterly sorry for the common herd who
could not appreciate His supreme art of dying.   Louis
Dubedat lived as a rake and died as an artist.   That
he would thus find high favour in his wife's eyes is
only to be expected.   Shaw points the moral that art
is a spiritual energy and cannot be spoiled by emerging
from a mind that is petty and calculating.   And he

does seem to suggest that, when all is said and done, doctors, although an apparent contradictory proposition, belong to a profession that is a picture of mankind using its abilities in the best way. I do not mean to say that Shaw approves of doctors as doctors, but that he approves of the spirit that lies behind sincere doctoring. For Shaw himself is something of a healer : he hits hard ; he flays with many lashes, but he does not rub salt in the wounds. Rather, he says —Look at your wounds ; see why they have been obtained ; do not let the necessity for them arise again ; do not take up your bed and walk ; sleep more soundly in it, that on the morrow you may understand more perfectly the wishes of the Life Force.

For we have now arrived at the central philosophy of Bernard Shaw—the valuable doctrine of the Life Force. We have been led up gently towards this position : Man fails but he fails with a purpose : he may slip backwards and backwards, but the top of the mountain is still there for him to reach : he is in the thick wood, but the wood has its way out. So we come to a discussion of Shaw's greatest play—*Man and Superman*, the play that is an expression of the two essential factors of the Shavian philosophy—the idea of the superman and the evolution of the doctrine that we are governed by a Life Force.

MAN, SUPERMAN, AND A WOMAN

IT is not always easy to realise that *Man and Superman* is a play at all. Shaw has taken considerable liberty with the dramatist's art and has written a deep philosophical discussion in the form of a play. If any proof were needed to show how brilliant is the Shavian dialogue, we should find it by noting that the speeches in *Man and Superman*, though at times desperately long, are not ever too long. Shaw has more to say in this play than in any other : it is quite surprising how much he manages to say that is true. He means to let us have it. It is your own fault, he seems to say, you have encouraged me by applauding my plays ; you have encouraged me more by your hostility to their sentiments ; now you shall have the full measure of what I really do think. I have talked about man : I shall now talk about the Devil; and God will now feel flattered that I am now going to say something about Him, but I shall call Him something else.

There are, of course, two main themes in *Man and Superman*. The one, easily the more important, is the doctrine of the Life Force ; the other, a new point of view that is older than the hills in reality, that woman in her pursuit of man is quite unscrupulous and does not pursue a man, but pursues the fulfilment of her own power of creation.   It is impossible in a chapter to do more than touch upon a certain number of Shavian positions that arise during the course of the play.   The plot is the simplest possible—the plot in which all humanity takes part.   John Tanner is determined not to be captured by Ann Whitefield. Ann is determined to capture John Tanner.   She does so.   Ann Whitefield is the new woman who was born when Adam was good-natured enough to allow his rib to be used for the making of her.   Tanner was born when God breathed on the dust.   Ann Whitefield and John Tanner were brought together when Shaw decided to give us his new point of view which has everything to recommend it except the fact that it is not new.   And it is no small part of the genius of Bernard Shaw that he manages to make many of the arguments in this play appear new.

Let us turn to a consideration of the play itself.

Tanner is a revolutionary who, like many revolutionaries, is convinced that he lives in a world that derides everything that is real.   There is a great deal of truth in this.   We do shun reality because it is beastly : we substitute in its place unreality which is often even more beastly.   Again, Tanner argues with a great deal of veracity that we suffer shame not because of the thing we do, but because we fear to do things that other people will see us do.   We do not ride in buses because we are ashamed to be seen in the same vehicle with people superior to ourselves. We are ashamed to read a bad book because we are ashamed to admit that we enjoy it so much more than a good one.   In Act I Tanner discusses with a

good deal of violence a very favourite position held
by Bernard Shaw—a position which ordinary society
never understands at all.   It is that uncompromising
and unscrupulous sincerity of the real artist. Tanner
argues at considerable length about the fact that
there is ever a fierce fight between the artist and his
art and the artist and his material responsibilities.
If the sacrifice of his wife makes a good picture, he
will sacrifice her : if the non-sacrifice of his wife
makes a better picture, he will not sacrifice her.
Tanner puts the whole inevitable conflict between the
real artist and his unreal view of life perfectly simply
and perfectly truly.   The artist will use everybody
and everything to the furtherance of his own art : he
will kill bodies and destroy souls that the soul of his
art may be more richly nourished.   And as a climax
Tanner is so devastatingly right when he insists on
the terrible struggle that there is between the artist
man and the mother woman.   He does not, of course,
see the possibility which is growing daily, that the
coming struggle is going to be between the artist
woman and the mother man, for more and more is
woman becoming convinced that she has as much
right as a man to put her own art of painting pictures
in front of the very commonplace and often very
pernicious art of motherhood.   Shaw, were he
younger, might well be expected to write a play and
call it not " Man and Superman," but " Man and
Superwoman."   But be that as it may—Shaw does
sum up admirably the horrid struggle that takes
place in a thousand homes, when the man wants to
paint a picture or write a book, and the woman

growls at him remorselessly—"unless you continue to
travel by the 8.35 I shall not be able to provide eggs
and bacon for my child." Fortunately for the continuance of life in the world there are not many true
artists living ! Here, then, is a Shavian picture of the
deplorable and inevitable warfare between the artist
and his worldly difficulties :

> TANNER. Since marriage began, the great artist
> has been known as a bad husband. But he is
> worse : he is a child robber, a blood-sucker, a
> hypocrite and a cheat. Perish the race and
> wither a thousand women if only the sacrifice of
> them enable him to act Hamlet better, to paint
> a finer picture, to write a deeper poem, a greater
> play, a profounder philosophy ! For, mark you,
> Tavy, the artist's work is to show us ourselves as
> we really are. Our minds are nothing but this
> knowledge of ourselves ; and he who adds a jot
> to such knowledge creates new knowledge as
> surely as any woman creates new men. In the
> rage of that creation he is as ruthless as the
> woman, as dangerous to her as she to him, and
> as horribly fascinating. Of all human struggles
> there is none so treacherous and remorseless as
> the struggle between the artist man and the
> mother woman. Which shall use up the other ?
> that is the issue between them. And it is all the
> deadlier because, in your romanticist cant, they
> love one another.

There is perhaps nothing very much to detain us in
Act I beyond a chance remark of Tanner which seems

to explain the destructive propensities of Bernard
Shaw. We must burn our old boats, otherwise we
shall never think about building new ones. Tanner
expresses also the hatred that Bernard Shaw seems to
have for institutions. He hates institutions because
they are a collective number of individuals who find it
very hard to be individualistic. There is a certain
half truth in this : a congregation in a church is a
collective number of individuals doing precisely the
same thing at a precise moment. But in essentials
they are as distinct individuals as though each member
of the congregation were worlds apart. Somehow
Shaw always seems to be too much afraid that institu-
tionalism is necessarily the opposite from free thought.
Quite often the very opposite is the case. Institution-
alism, far from curbing the individual, gives him a
feeling of security in matters that affect society as a
whole, so that, feeling his position in the community
is safe, he can give his full measure of energy to his
own particular tastes. But there is, I feel, a tremendous amount of truth in the Shavian assertion that
woman believes that destruction can only destroy.
It would be as well that woman could have charge of
our politicians when they intend to make war and
shut them up quietly in crêches while a female
parliament gets on with the work of the world. In a
larger issue, however, woman undoubtedly does view
the principle of destruction as being the principle of
destroying. Thus Ann quite naturally can see no
good in the revolutionary ideals of Tanner. She sees
him a destructive force tearing down things. She
will not look closely enough to see whether he is tearing

down illusions which have disillusioned the race for centuries.   Man in destroying Christ destroyed the God-man that he might build up God.   Ann cannot see that destruction quite often is the prelude to construction.   She does not see the vile slum being razed to the ground that there may be raised in its place a fine street.   She admits quite frankly that she cannot see beyond the crash and clash of destruction ; she can hear the ponderous blows of the destroying hammer, she cannot hear the ponderous blows that are putting foundations into the right place.   Thus we find the inevitable clash between the feminine and the masculine mind which is, after all, merely the symbol of race preservation.

ANN. I am afraid I am too feminine to see any sense in destruction.   Destruction can only destroy.

TANNER. Yes, that is why it is so useful.   Construction cumbers the ground with institutions made by busybodies.   Destruction clears it and gives us breathing space and liberty.

ANN. It's no use, Jack.   No woman will agree with you there.

TANNER. That's because you confuse construction and destruction with creation and murder. They're quite different : I adore creation and abhor murder.   Yes, I adore it in tree and flower, in bird and beast, even in you.   It was the creative instinct that led you to attach me to you by bonds that have left their mark on me to this day.   Yes, Ann ; the old childish compact between us was an unconscious love compact——

In Act II Shaw bursts out into a righteous rage. He always has something of that dislike of mothers which seems to be part of the make-up of an agitator. Tanner works himself up into a fit of bad temper. What, demands he, is the usual mother ? Nothing but a foul-minded old woman, who corrupts the minds of her daughters that they may prepare themselves for the best possible social marriage match. It is undoubtedly true that most mothers who happen to belong to the upper classes are quite naturally concerned with the desirability of gaining a good son-in-law who has good prospects. About this Shaw is very angry. Well, after all, most women are better women when they have money than when they have not. A husband who can wear silk pyjamas is less repulsive than one who is obliged to go about in woollen ones. We do see quite often, it is true, ambitious mothers who do not much care whom their daughters marry so long as there is position and money, but on the whole mother-made marriages are in the minority. And Shaw, I think, exaggerates the evil, and as feminine emancipation grows wider and wider we shall see less and less of the marriages that are made by ambitious mothers who would be appalled to be called mercenary scoundrels. Shaw gibes at fashionable society with a violent fury—that it reduces marriage to a mere business contract. But it is as well to remember that fashionable society is simply the polish of the world and does not constitute in the smallest degree the real mass of mankind. Fashionable society is only fashionable in society, and society, for the most part, is quite oblivious of non-

H

society. It looks upon it as something that is necessary but as far removed as though it dwelt on another
planet.

It will now be convenient to go for an interesting
excursion with Shaw and spend a quite delightful
week-end in hell, though I am bound to admit that,
for many people, the change would not be apparent.

.   .   .   .   .   .

We can pass over Shaw's gibe about the old Catholic
woman finding herself in hell. Instead we may pass
on to some excellent fooling that is a prelude to the
serious discussion that is the essence of *Man and
Superman*. The old Catholic lady is a little surprised
and annoyed to find that her servants in Hell will be
devils. The dialogue is a very good example of Shaw
in an ironic mood. The old lady has expressed her
disgust that in hell she is nobody at all, when on
earth we can quite well imagine that she can well
have lived in the Manor House.

> DON JUAN. Not at all; you are a lady; and
> wherever ladies are is hell. Do not be surprised
> or terrified; you will find everything here that
> a lady can desire, including devils who will serve
> you from sheer love of servitude, and magnify
> your importance for the sake of dignifying their
> service—the best of servants.

> THE OLD WOMAN. My servants will be devils!

> DON JUAN. Have you ever had servants who were
> not devils?

> THE OLD WOMAN. Never; they were devils, per-

fect devils, all of them. I thought you meant
that my servants here would be real devils.

DON JUAN. No more real devils than you will be
a real lady. Nothing is real here. That is the
horror of damnation.

Although it is not perhaps particularly important
what Shaw thinks about hell, his argument that it is
a place where the only thing to do is to live for
amusement is not without its amusing side. For
Shaw points out that one of the main advantages of
being in hell is that we have left hope behind, consequently it matters not at all what we do and it
matters not at all what we do not do. So the Statue
warns Ann, who has managed to find hell a little
overpowering, on no account to pray. It is interesting as depicting Shaw adopting that half-serious
tone which has made him puzzle so very many
excellent people who cannot determine whether he is
naughty or good, or merely Shaw. The answer is, of
course, that he is merely Shaw and is quite certain
that the best way to preach a sermon is by puzzling
his hearers and making them so rapidly angry and
good-tempered that they are forced ever to marshal
their mental forces and ask themselves, Well, what
on earth does Shaw really mean? And the answer is
that he really does mean what he says.

THE STATUE. No, no, no, my child ; do not pray.
If you do, you will throw away the main advantage of this place. Written over the gate here
are the words, " Leave every hope behind, ye
who enter." Only think what a relief that is !

For what is hope ? A form of moral responsibility.
Here there is no hope, and consequently no duty,
no work, nothing to be gained by praying, nothing to be lost by doing what you like. Hell,
in short, is a place where you have nothing to do
but amuse yourself. You sigh, friend Juan ;
but if you dwelt in heaven, as I do, you would
realise your advantages.

Before turning to the question of the Life Force,
we cannot leave on one side the delightful reason that
Shaw gives us as to why the Devil left heaven. It is,
we are told, quite simply, that the Devil was bored
with living in heaven. And there is not the slightest
doubt but that the conventional idea of heaven is
that it is a very boring place. Shaw is, of course,
obviously tilting at the popular conception of heaven,
though, as a matter of fact, the Church teaching with
regard to heaven tends to become more and more
vague and unsatisfactory. We have evolved from
the Middle Ages theology depicting a kind of royal
palace heaven, to a theology which now seems content
with the rather doubtful assertion that we make our
own heaven in a sort of way that suggests the possession of an energy over which we have sufficient power
to turn it into either heaven or hell. While God
looks on and wonders what He has done to have lost
all His power ! And Shaw himself seems to fall in
line with the mystical thinkers who demand that
heaven is a kind of mental energy, when he remarks
that, after all, heaven is a matter of temperament.
The discussion on heaven leads us quite naturally to

the consideration of the Life Force, the real discussion concerning which begins when Don Juan admits that his main ambition, although he is a revolutionary, is to help man upwards and onwards. We are now entering upon the fundamental philosophy of Bernard Shaw. We are witnessing him concerned with the appalling fact that the witness of history is that man has been not so much a villain as a blunderer, the worst form of villainy. This, then, is the vision that confronts Don Juan and it is to be his heaven to see the Life Force working itself towards the goal it would wish to attain.

The real grievance that Bernard Shaw has against man is that he is so wonderful, indeed, the lord of all creation; but he makes so little of himself. Shaw sees a horrid and a desperate fight in which man creates, as it were, difficulties by reason of his stupidity and ignorance. Yet not only is man possessed of the best power of understanding himself: he for some extraordinary reason seems to possess very poor brains. He is the most intensely alive thing, and yet how dead. He has organised life and yet is but the tool of a brute system. His natural place is in the wide, open countryside; yet he crowds together in masses and lives in an atmosphere in which the sun never sets because it never rises. So vile is the world which man has created that stupidity has been driven into being sordid and cruel. Thus Don Juan cries out the accusation that Shaw delivers against mankind.

Don Juan. Stupidity made sordid and cruel by the realities learnt from toil and poverty: Imagina-

tion resolved to starve sooner than face these
realities, piling up illusions to hide them, and
calling itself cleverness, genius ! And each accusing the other of its own defect : Stupidity
accusing Imagination of folly, and Imagination
accusing Stupidity of ignorance ; whereas, alas !
Stupidity has all the knowledge, and Imagination
all the intelligence.

Now it is quite obvious that Shaw does not believe
that the superman need necessarily be big of body.
For, asks Don Juan, have we not tried animals of
colossal stature only to find that their brain power has
been so feeble that they have not been able to save
themselves from destruction. This, then, is the
argument put forward by Don Juan, to which the
Devil retorts at vast length. After all, granted that
man has a superior brain to the beasts of the field or
the fowls of the air or the fishes in the sea, has he been
any better able to prevent himself from being destroyed ? He declares himself to be cleverer than
nature ; he produces plague; he has riddled himself
with cancer ; he has so muddled the sex relations
that they produce the most foul disease ; he has
turned his back on common-sense and cursed God as
a fool. In war he has turned his intellectual energies
to the direction of destroying his enemies by the very
weapons he has himself condemned. The marvellous
Life Force that he boasts of is but the force of death.
What is his religion ? Merely an excuse for hating the
Devil. What is his law ? Merely an excuse for
hanging people who are a little bit troublesome.

What is his morality ? To be accounted well in the
world : to walk down the village street and not be
found out : to cloak all his sins and camouflage them
as virtues. What is his sport ? The hunting of
animals so that taking part in a perfectly safe sport
he can consider himself a hero. What are his politics ? Either deadly fear of a tyrannical monster or
the spectacle of many of the most inefficient men in
the country fighting those who are even more inefficient. So the Devil goes on in his indictment of
mankind. What is our conception of political
economy ? To spend a million pounds on the construction of battleships and squabble over two pounds
that may be spent to prevent a tuberculous family
from all sleeping together in the same bed. What
has been the history of man ? A history in which
ecclesiastical tyranny has preached the love of God
by means of the rack and the thumbscrew. What,
concludes the Devil, after all, is man ? Nothing but
a clever and unscrupulous destroyer. He has been
" the inventor of the rack, the stake, the gallows, and
the electrocutor ; of the sword and gun ; above all,
of justice, duty, patriotism, and all the other isms
by which even those who are clever enough to be
humanely disposed are persuaded to become the
most destructive of all the destroyers." To which
Don Juan replies with shattering truth that mankind
does not mind how much it is slated provided you do
not call it a coward.

And Bernard Shaw quite unfairly, I think, is of the
opinion that all our civilisation is really based on
cowardice, which we call for our own sakes respect-

ability. For once Shaw is desperately conventional.
It is the height of conventionality to consider that
respectability is mere cowardice. We are always
hearing perfectly nice and sincere people say with a
great show of alleged broadmindedness that we are
good because we are afraid to be bad, that we postulate immortality because we are afraid of extinction,
that we are in favour of legitimate children because
we are afraid of illegitimate children—in a word, that
our sincerity is merely a form of cowardice. Such a
position is quite certainly fallacious. There are undoubtedly many people who are good because it pays :
there are quite certainly many more who are not
because it does not pay. What Bernard Shaw nearly
always seems to find it impossible to contemplate is
the possibility (the age of miracles not having passed
even in this modern age) of the discovery of the
disinterested person. We are not all respectable
because we are cowards. We are not all libertines
because we are bold men. We are respectable because we do think quite often that, as the Greeks
thought, a respectable way of living is likely to be for
most of us in harmony with what our natures were
meant to be.

There is, of course, a tremendous truth in the
assertion that we are braver when fighting for other
people than when fighting for ourselves. We will
fight with the utmost bravery for our brother's
morality, but the same night we will have a vulgar
intrigue with a prostitute. It is again true, as Shaw
says, that the Crusader was braver than the pirate
because he fought for the Cross and not for himself.

And it is also, I think, very important when Shaw points out that if it is true that the Crusader was brave on behalf of the Cross, the Mohammedans were equally brave on behalf of the cause of Islam. For we are always inclined to think that the bravery of the Christian is superior to that of the non-Christian, whereas the point that Shaw would make is that the principle of fighting for any kind of cause induces an excellent principle of courage.

But even so, while Shaw admits that man can be brave for an idea, he soon disqualifies the virtue by declaring, with all that enthusiasm with which he suddenly smashes a pleasant position, that if a man on the one hand will fight for an idea like a hero, on the other he will also develop into a dangerous fanatic.

So Don Juan takes us up to the actual idea of the Life Force. And Shaw has been gently leading us up to the position that the Life Force is a power behind man. Man for a while has to go his own way. He falls again and again : his mistakes are as numerous as the sands of the desert : he is as ruffled as the sea on a rough day. But behind all his terrible errors there is a fundamental striving for something he does not quite understand. He is striving, probably unconsciously, that he may understand what it is that the Life Force wishes him to do. We feel all the time that Shaw is of the opinion that the Life Force knows what it wants and knows that at present man cannot interpret its wishes. For the Life Force (though I believe that Shaw believes that it could) will not force man. Man must learn by his mistakes. Let him stroll through the darkest forest : one day he will find the road that leads him out. Let man decimate himself by cancer and consumption : one day he shall be as clean as the cleansed leper. Let him make ten thousand wars : let him invent energy which will destroy a city before the cock crows thrice —one day he will see that the star of peace will break up the darkness of war.

> DON JUAN. My point, you marble-headed old masterpiece, is only a step ahead of you. Are we agreed that Life is a force which has made innumerable experiments in organising itself ; that the mammoth and the man, the mouse and the megatherium, the flies and the fleas and the Fathers of the Church, are all more or less successful attempts to build up that raw force into higher and higher individuals, the ideal individual being omnipotent, omniscient, infallible, and withal completely, unilludèdly self-conscious : in short, a god ?

The argument that the Life Force must have a brain is a convincing position. There are many of us who would be inclined to agree with the Statue that we might well expect to enjoy life without thinking about it. And we should certainly also agree that more often than not thinking about life destroys any pleasure we may get out of it. Don Juan remarks with a great deal of understanding that the intellect is decidedly unpopular. It is unpopular. The masses of the people do not want to think and it is, of course, fortunate for the leaders of the masses that they do not want to think. Thought is disliked because thought is ever a breaking up. But, as Shaw would point out, intellect is necessary to man so that he may avoid blunders and come to know and be able to carry out the wishes of the Life Force. And, says Bernard Shaw, do we not see that life is ever a series of painful experiments, a rough road of learning that gradually leads to the construction of an instrument of defence? Take the eye, says Bernard Shaw. Life has evolved it after centuries of struggle, so that man can see where he is going, avoid that which would destroy him, gain keener sight of that which will help him. Thus, letting life be analogous to the eye, life is evolving a mind's eye, "that shall see not the physical world, but the purpose of life and thereby enable the individual to work for that purpose instead of thwarting and baffling it by setting up short-sighted personal aims as at present."

We now come to what I may call the *particular* part of *Man and Superman*. It is the struggle that Tanner puts up against Ann, well knowing all the time that it is a fight against the inevitable. For, as Shaw insists, Tanner is fighting against an impersonal force. When he attempts to fight against the fascination of Ann, he is not fighting against a person but against a creative force that is universal and unscrupulous. For whether they wish it or not, two people (who are interested in one another) of the opposite sex are mere particles of dust blown about by a violent current of emotion which is simply using them as pawns. The Life Force requiring another person through which to make more experiments, merely chooses out two persons who, perfectly un-

conscious that they are mere pawns, fly into each
other's arms. And to the joy of all the commonplace
relations they produce a new pawn for the Life
Force's experiment. So Shaw leads up to the perfectly sensible position that the sex relation is entirely
universal and will admit of no question of insularity
or birth or creed. We can no more help so-called
sexual immorality than we can avoid death. We are
always told that Christ was sexually pure : there is
no reason whatever to doubt that this was so. But
we surely do not outrage any reasonable person by
suggesting that the reason Christ was sexually pure
was that He was the universal Spirit and therefore
could not be the servant of any kind of energy. For
the participants in the sex relation are servants : they
are merely obeying the implacable commands of the
Life Force. Multiply on the earth, said God in the
Old Testament. Sex relationship is impersonal, says
Shaw in *Man and Superman*. More and more are we
beginning to realize that sex speaks all languages, is
curbed by no creed, will express itself in the desert or
in the crowded city, will become active in the stinking
garret or the gilded salon of the demi-monde. And
yet, while we would agree with Bernard Shaw that
the sex relation is simply an expression of that
universal creative force implanted in man, we do not
discover him dealing with the unpleasant fact that
many of our sex relationships produce nothing at all
and are rapidly becoming merely the logical termina-
tion to an excellent day on the river. In fact, one is
bound to say that if the Life Force is looking for new
experimenters by means of its preconceived plan of

throwing the opposite sexes together, it must experience many and vast disappointments.

> DON JUAN. In the sex relation the universal creative energy, of which the parties are both the helpless agents, over-rides and sweeps away all personal relations. The pair may be utter strangers to one another, speaking different languages, differing in race and colour, in age and disposition, with no bond between them but a possibility of that fecundity for the sake of which the Life Force throws them into one another's arms at the exchange of a glance.

A little later on Don Juan with a good deal of cunning argues that his intentions towards women were much more honourable because he did not offer them marriage than those of the man who offered them marriage and expected in return most of their property. The libertine does, of course, expect much less from a woman than the married man. In fact, Don Juan remarks with a good deal of cynical truth that he found that when a woman displayed an interest in him, he had either to take to flight or become a slave to the end of his life. Shaw is, of course, beginning to touch on the marriage problem, but as I deal with that problem exclusively in my next chapter, there is no need to pursue the argument further here.

Close to the end of Act III Ann expresses her whole philosophy and, I fancy, a good deal of Shaw's own philosophy of womanhood, when she exclaims with an almost religious enthusiasm that her desire is to secure a mate who will be the father of the superman. Thus the whole unscrupulousness of woman is brought out, that she merely cares for man in so far as he is the instrument for producing the superchild —in other words, the potential superman.

THE STATUE. Good. All the same, the Superman is a fine conception. There is something statuesque about it. Ah, this reminds me of old times.

THE DEVIL. And me also.

ANA. Stop!

THE DEVIL. You, Señora, cannot come this way. You will have an apotheosis. But you will be at the palace before us.

ANA. That is not what I stopped you for. Tell me: where can I find the Superman?

THE DEVIL. He is not yet created, Señora.

THE STATUE. And never will be, probably. Let us proceed; the red fire will make me sneeze.

ANA. Not yet created! Then my work is not yet done. I believe in the Life to Come. A father —a father for the Superman!

So at the end of the play Tanner capitulates to Ann. The Life Force has really tricked him: the Life Force has made Ann so attractive that Tanner cannot resist her. Thus he remarks despairingly, "The Life Force enchants me: I have the whole world in my arms when I clasp you." Shaw is here so amazingly accurate. For the moment the loved one does seem to be the whole universe, but it is not long before we discover that the loved one is no real part of the universe at all, but a trap set for us by the cunning Life Force.

.   .   .   .   .

Man and Superman is acknowledged by most people to be Shaw's masterpiece.   I see no reason to disagree with such an opinion.   The play is a very definite and skilfully reasoned philosophy.   Those who condemn Shaw as a pessimist for his positions in this play sadly fail to see that the underlying principle of the whole work is a very definite and unhesitating optimism. Man is engaged upon the quest of understanding what it is that he is meant to do, so that his manhood may be perfect and the most utilitarian.   Shaw gradually leads us up to the question of a superman and a super-race.   Man will be his own saviour : by his repeated mistakes he will learn the wishes of the Life Force, carry them out more and more accurately and thus in time raise himself up to be a Superman of whom the Life Force will be proud.

Chapter III

SHAW AND MARRIAGE

IN his preface on marriage, Shaw has a great many interesting things to say and some of them are ordinary enough to be useful! Shaw deals with the problem of marriage with a toleration that is a little surprising. The ideal is not free love but love that is free. Marriage so often enslaves love turning it into a dull respectability or, in extreme cases, a violent hatred.

It is as well to make it quite clear that Shaw sees marriage to be for all practical purposes inevitable. There are, and always will be, those who ignore the marriage convention (and quite a reasonable convention) and take the law into their own hands, only to find more often than not, that it rapidly passes out of their hands. Some will live together and the pseudo wedding ring will do duty for the real one. Others will quite openly declare that they intend to defy convention only to discover that the conventional, being too strong, will not be aware of their existence. So much nonsense has been talked about Shaw's attitude to marriage that it is as well to put on paper his fundamental position. What we have got to do, he demands, is not to get a substitute for marriage, but not to let marriage be conducted in such a manner that it becomes a substitute for

118

common sense. Marriage is the normal state ; illicit
unions are abnormal. Shaw never wishes to legislate
for the abnormal. They are quite capable of looking
after themselves, and if they are not, those who are
normal will see to it that they do not become a
nuisance.

"Marriage remains practically inevitable ; and
the sooner we acknowledge this, the sooner we
shall set to work to make it decent and reasonable."

Here, then, is the Shavian ambition, to make
marriage better, to make it the reasonable contract it
was meant to be, to strip it of those illusions which
make the marriage state so full of misery and disappointment. In this chapter I shall endeavour to
deal with a few of the Shavian suggestions for im-
proving marriage. And no doubt if we live long
enough we shall find that some of them will be
adopted, but opinion will, I am afraid, be too biassed
to attribute the changes to Shaw.

.   .   .   .   .

A good deal of water has flowed under London
Bridge since Shaw wrote his preface on marriage.
Westminster has seen so many changes that it can
hardly be aware of how far-reaching they are. The
most far-reaching has been the vote given to women
whether they have the intelligence of nursemaids or
the morals of Mayfair. The result has been something which Shaw might have anticipated—there has

I

been, and is, a new thinking about marriage. And it is a new thinking that is pretty old thinking to Shaw, for he deals with the question in the preface I am examining. He discusses something that he calls the new attack on marriage and it is just this— that a large number of people are sensible enough to have marriage and let the other people have the children.

From one point of view the enemy of marriage is not now the libertine but the married woman. It is against her that the pious (who are always the un-practical people) launch their attack. She is the arch-villain because she prefers to keep her figure rather than stroll down Balham High Street with four shrieking children. She is no longer deluded by the vulgar nonsense that marriage was meant for children. There is a growing movement for birth control and women are no longer conscious of being loved by God if they spend the best years of their lives in lying-in hospitals. What, then, is this attack on marriage that Bernard Shaw prophesied so long ago? It is that marriage is becoming the most licentious institution possible. There is nothing new in this—it always has been so. But it is new to find a more or less official attack being made on the respectably married as being licentious, instead of praising them as representing an antidote against libertine licentiousness.

Thus Bernard Shaw tells us of the alleged new attack which is being launched against marriage— that the hand which rules the world refuses to rock the cradle.

" The Fictitious Free Lover, who was supposed
to attack marriage because it thwarted his in-
ordinate affection and prevented him from
making life a carnival, has vanished and given
place to the very real, very strong, very austere
avenger of outraged decency who declares that
the licentiousness of marriage now that it no
longer recruits the race, is destroying it."

In other words marriage is merely the means to an
end and is of no importance intrinsically.

At this stage I must deal briefly with Shaw's
consideration of what he chooses to call, no doubt
gloating over a somewhat commonplace paradox, the
religious revolt against marriage. He remarks that,
to this day, " the celibacy of the Roman Catholic
priesthood is a standing protest against its com-
patibility with the higher life." This is a disastrous
misunderstanding of the real attitude of the Church
towards marriage. The Catholic Church never by
any chance says that marriage is not compatible with
the higher life, whatever this may mean. What it
does say, and says with great emphasis, is that in
effect a priest cannot serve two masters—God and a
wife. There is no suggestion that priests are to
eschew marriage because it is an intimate association
with a woman, but they are to eschew marriage
because their relation with God is so intimate that it
is, to put it quite crudely, a full-time job. Again,
Shaw talks with a considerable show of an uncritical
attitude of St. Paul's reluctant sanction of marriage.
Whereas, if the Pauline epistles are read with any

degree of scholarly acumen, it becomes quite obvious that what St. Paul is driving at is that, to put it into modern language, we must not rush into marriage without thinking about the vocational side of it. Shaw does seem to take the view that St. Paul had a certain contempt for the married state—a position that so many moderns assume in their frenzied efforts to try to show that the teaching of St. Paul on marriage is not only out of date but almost unmoral. It is a little surprising to find Shaw led by the nose in this manner, and, for the moment, one of the cheap-jack thinkers, who are always forgetting that the Epistles happen to have been written in Greek, and that they happen to be written by God and therefore may be expected to be free from printer's errors.

And Shaw writes this really extraordinary observation concerning the apparent fear that ministers of religion experience when they behold the married people in their parishes suffering, as he puts it, much more from intemperance than many of the known libertines. Somehow, Shaw seems to miss the point. While the Church, on the one hand, quite logically condemns the childless marriage, she will always condemn much more roundly the child that is born outside marriage. And it is nonsense to say that the married people of a village or town live a less satisfactory life than those who have no sense of morality and no sense of reasonable control.

Let us turn to an interesting discussion that marriage cannot expect to produce a love all the time. What Shaw says in effect is that we must be on guard

against marriage becoming a bore to ourselves and a
bore to our neighbours. And there is no doubt
whatever that boredom is a terrible destroyer of
marriage. The husband is bored with his wife, and
it is not long before he realises that boredom is a
deadly ally with adultery. The wife is bored when
her husband returns from the non-making of money
in the city; boredom is driving her towards the
divorce court.

So Shaw warns us against the people who declare
that the ideal marriage cannot be attained unless we
are desperately in love twenty-four hours every day
and three hundred and sixty-five days every year.
Thus he writes only too truly:

> " The people who talk and write as if the high-
> est attainable state is that of a family stewing in
> love continuously from the cradle to the grave,
> can hardly have given five minutes' serious con-
> sideration to so outrageous a proposition."

And Shaw goes on to say, only too truly, that the
logical application of such a preposterous proposition
will show itself in that disastrous boredom, the
deplorable results of which I have already emphasised.

> "A wife entirely preoccupied with her affection
> for her husband, a mother entirely preoccupied
> with her affection for her children, may be all
> very well in a book (for people who like that kind
> of book); but in actual life she is a nuisance."

There is a very great deal of truth in the rather

melancholy fact which Shaw stresses, of the impossibility of two people, although married, knowing
anything at all about one another. We never do
know another person. For a whole year we may
sleep with the same person in the same bed and yet
know all too well that all we know of the other person
is what the other person chooses to let us know. We
may occupy the same sheets but we cannot read
between the lines. And the further part of the whole
tragic affair is that however much another person
wishes us to know him, we only succeed in discerning
our own picture of what the other person wishes us
to know. We cannot read the unexpressed thoughts
and the expressed thoughts probably do not express
what they really mean. No, our marriage partner
is a stranger and we know him best only when he is
dead. Shaw is, of course, rather pessimistic about
this non-knowing of the marriage partner, but I am
afraid he is quite right.

"The majority of married couples never get to
know one another at all : they only get accustomed to having the same house, the same
children, and the same income, which is quite a
different matter. The comparatively few men
who work at home—writers, artists, and, to
some extent, clergymen—have to effect some
sort of segregation within the house or else run
a heavy risk of overstraining their domestic
relations. When the pair is so poor that it can
afford only a single room, the strain is intolerable :
violent quarrelling is the result. Very few

couples can live in a single-roomed tenement without exchanging blows quite frequently.''

It is quite worth while to spend a little time in considering Shaw's attitude to the popular idea that marriage is a kind of magic spell. So many people do imagine that marriage not only binds two people but changes them. Nothing is more foolish. The man who, before marriage, is a grumpy, small-souled little ass, is, after marriage, a small-souled, grumpy little ass. The woman who has a horde of admirers before marriage, is desperately annoyed if she finds, after marriage, that her only admirer is her husband. Marriage does not change people except for the worse! Shaw writes only too truly :

"Also, there is no *hocus-pocus* that can possibly be devised with rings and veils and vows and benedictions that can fix either a man's or woman's affection for twenty minutes, much less twenty years.''

Far from changing people, as Shaw argues, marriage leaves them as they were, or, in the bad cases, induces a change for the worse. We say glibly enough that we shall love a person for ever, forgetting that it would be so much wiser to say it *after* the marriage night. Love is blind and, whether we wish it or not, we too soon recover our sight. Sex makes marriage, and sex unmakes marriage. We so frequently seem to miss this, and it all leads up to the unfortunate fact that, as we were before our great day, so we are afterwards ; and perhaps death is like marriage—we are the same after as before. The more we recognise

that marriage does not change us in the way that a
fairy can turn a pig into a fairy prince and a sow into
a fairy princess, the more shall we make a success of
marriage : for we shall expect little and we shall not
be disappointed.

> "The people who are quarrelsome quarrel with
> their husbands and wives just as easily as with
> their servants and relatives and acquaintances ;
> marriage makes no difference."

I do not propose to go into the question of the unscrupulous and yet unconscious weapon of sex
attraction, which is dealt with at some length by
Bernard Shaw. We all know that, without being in
the least flippant, sex is a trap that the world may
go on, whether it deserves to or not.

Let us consider very briefly the excellent little
Shavian attack on the abominable lack of manners
that most of us display in our own homes. The old
music-hall gag that "those two cannot be married
because they are so polite to one another," has a
horrible amount of truth in it. We walk into the
drawing-room of a mere casual acquaintance, having
spent ten minutes wiping the mud off our boots : we
walk into our own drawing-room so that our wives
have to spend three hours getting the mud off the
carpet. Why should we be knights in the outside
circle and cads in the inner circle ? Because in nine
cases out of ten, whether we want it or not, familiarity
does breed contempt. We will cheerfully, in matters
of sex, treat the marriage partner with a lack of
consideration that we would not give to a common

street prostitute. Observe every decency in single life : observe none in married life—such is the popular feeling. Our bodies are temples of the Holy Ghost, but let them be treated with every coarseness so long as we are respectably married. So Shaw attacks pretty strongly the people who reserve the genius of their bad manners for their own homes :

> "If such people took their domestic manners into general society, they would very soon find themselves without a friend or even an acquaintance in the world."

We are gradually leading up to the question of divorce. One of the minor difficulties of marriage is that we are more or less expected to like the marriage partner. Imagination cannot create a greater monster than he who does not like his wife. There is no more deadly sin, unless you are a sincere Bohemian, than saying that your husband is as dull as most men. Society, which will always pardon the most successful sin, but never the most successful failure, is outraged when two married people disagree, because Society hates to see the inadequacy of its own rules. So Bernard Shaw points out that not only do married people have to put up with the ill-manners of the other party, but that they are expected to love and honour those whom, in ordinary life, they would turn out of the door. Two people who cordially dislike each other are expected by Society to eat, drink, sleep and snore together. They must display a mutual interest in each other's business, while heading towards rapid matrimonial bankruptcy. It is, of course, true that the natural emotion between husband and wife is one of affection. But it is really too bad of us to expect two people to make a show of affection just for the sake of appearances, when the affection has departed. Therefore we have now arrived at a time when we may consider quite logically something of Bernard Shaw's attitude to divorce.

.   .   .   .   .

Continual surprise is being expressed at the prevalence of divorce. No surprise is ever expressed at the prevalence of non-divorce, and considering that marriage is, after all, asking two strangers to live perfectly unnatural lives, it says a great deal for human nature that marriage endures as well as it does. We are always so intrigued by the number of divorce cases that we entirely forget to ask what percentage of marriages do *not* end in divorce. It would be still more interesting to ask how many years prior to the separation of the marriage partners by death have elapsed since the marriage to all intents and purposes ceased to be a marriage in the ideal sense at all. Quite simply Bernard Shaw demands that there is really only one valid reason for divorce and that is that the people in question want one.

A heavy body of opinion (of which, of course, the Church is the main supporter) desire that, when two married people have grown tired of each other, they shall exercise a certain amount of courage and continue to make the best of a bad job. Leaving on one side the Church's argument that marriage is a sacrament and therefore indissoluble, let us ask whether there

is any practical benefit in forcing two ill-assorted
people to live together in unholy matrimony. From
the point of view of affection we shall witness a couple
living a downright lie : from the economic standpoint
that divorce may rob the state of children, we shall
probably find an ill-assorted union producing children
ill-conditioned and undesirable. Now Shaw reverses
the whole position. Whereas it is considered by the
Church and a large section of secular opinion moral
for two ill-assorted people to continue to live together
in marriage, Shaw demands that it is a gross piece of
immorality to expect them to do so. And there is a
great deal to be said for what he says. For let us
speak with all possible plainness. In asking people
who desire to be divorced to continue to live together,
we are asking a couple to take part in a life of dis-
harmony which may at the one end result in continual
bickering, while at the other may quite conceivably
develop into nothing less than legitimate rape. So
Shaw writes angrily of what he considers to be the
folly of forcing a continuance of the married state on
those who no longer wish it.

> " To impose marriage on two unmarried people
> who do not desire to marry one another would
> be admittedly an act of enslavement. But it is
> no worse than to impose a continuation of mar-
> riage on people who have ceased to desire to be
> married."

Now Bernard Shaw supports his arguments for
divorce by enunciating with a considerable amount of
emphasis the idea prevalent amongst so-called

advanced thinkers—that divorce strengthens marriage. He supports his theory with a very simple illustration. All he says, in effect, is simply this :

> " A thousand divorces may mean two thousand marriages ; for the couples may marry again."

But unfortunately the problem is not by any means so easily solved. Divorce may injure marriage by making people feel that there is, after all, a way out. On the other hand, it may act as an auxiliary to marriage by inducing a large number of people to risk marriage who would undoubtedly never marry if they knew the bonds to be inevitably sealed until death. What, of course, all thinkers should aim at is the production of a society which will handle its marriages so well that *ipso facto* divorce will be non-existent. But we must take things as they are. At present, in my opinion, divorce is as inevitable as marriage is inevitable. We shall only get rid of divorce when we have made every marriage (as it is meant to be) a reasonable companionship and not, as so many think it, some kind of magic rite which turns men and women into perfect puppets.

It is as well to remember all through that in dealing with marriage Bernard Shaw quite evidently does not recognise any sacramental nature of the rite. The arguments that he puts forward, therefore, can only be considered outside the Church's teaching about marriage. I do not see that his arguments can have any weight at all with a churchman of any kind, except in so far, of course, as they parallel themselves to a line of action that would not be condemned by

the Church. So he writes as a kind of summing up
to the whole question of divorce and marriage, thus :

> "The notion that there is or ever can be any-
> thing magical and inviolable in the legal relations
> of domesticity, and the curious confusion of ideas
> which makes some of our bishops imagine that
> in the phrase ' Whom God hath joined ' the
> word God means the district registrar or the
> Reverend John Smith or William Jones, must be
> got rid of. Means of breaking up undesirable
> families are as necessary to the preservation of
> the family as means of dissolving undesirable
> marriages are to the preservation of marriage.
> If our domestic laws are kept so inhuman that
> they at last provoke a furious general insurrec-
> tion against them as they already provoke many
> private ones, we shall in a very literal sense
> empty the baby out with the bath by abolishing
> an institution which needs nothing more than a
> little obvious and easy rationalising to make it
> not only harmless but comfortable, honourable,
> and useful."

.   .   .   .   .

I have not dealt with the play *Getting Married* as
most of the arguments in it can be found in the
preface and they are there more seriously discussed.
Whether we agree with Bernard Shaw in his conclusions or whether we do not, we shall at least find
it valuable to give thought to his various points of
view. His sincerity is emphatic all through. Mar-

riage must be marriage and not a make-believe. We must have no false sentiments about marriage : when it fails divorce must step in. We shall not arrive at a better state of affairs by refusing to look things in the face even if the vision afforded is unpleasant. Marriage is one of the experiments set man by the Life Force. At present he has not made the best of it. The Life Force would certainly regard divorce as a failure, but would be sensible enough to say that while your marriage state is imperfect, divorce cannot be left out of the picture. When those who are about to marry understand fully the wishes of the Life Force they will produce marriage as it should be, and be in a better position to bring forth a super-race, who will not be men masquerading as gods, but men understanding God and thereby understanding themselves. Go in, says Shaw, and work for better conditions of marriage. Listen to what the Life Force wants : try to carry it out, and ye shall become as men knowing good and evil, and men who will choose the good. And thus will you produce after many attempts the ideal state of marriage which will be equally satisfying both to man and woman.

PART III

BERNARD SHAW AND CHRISTIANITY

BERNARD SHAW AND CHRISTIANITY

HAD Shaw not chosen to be a playwright I am
sure he would have been a theologian. He is
always intensely interested in man and is equally
interested in God. Now there is a peculiar value in a
playwright dealing with any organised religion, for he
will view it dispassionately. But it may be argued
that, since Bernard Shaw chose to base one of his
plays on a discussion of Christianity, he might be
expected to view the Creed not dispassionately but
with due regard to the box office. Such an argument
would fail, as do all arguments which accuse an
intensely sincere person of turning anything to his
own account. Shaw has quite obviously written a
frank criticism of Christianity and Christ. On the
one hand there is no reason why Christ should not
be criticised because He happens to have been a
pre-eminent Person. On the other hand the orthodox, who see in a criticism of Him a kind of blatant
blasphemy, have to explain how a Being who is above
criticism can be criticised. Assuming for a moment
that, unlike most teachers, Christ really meant what
He said, there is no particular reason why Shaw
should not criticise God, except perhaps that it is
rather a waste of time.

In this part we have to deal as fully as we can in

K

a more or less confined space with some of the points
that Shaw raises concerning Christ. Their main
importance is, perhaps, that Shaw happens to be a
public figure and most public figures have something
interesting to say about religion. Shaw commences
his consideration of Christianity by giving us a rather
cheap epigram that perhaps explains in a way why
he never realised his own peculiar Christological position. Thus Shaw writes with that curious kind of
vagueness which assails the creedless man who feels
robbed of something that might be worth having :
" We have always had a curious feeling that though
we crucified Christ on a stick, He somehow managed
to get hold of the right end of it, and that if we were
better men we might try His plan. "Now I cannot
help feeling, somehow, that in some way Shaw has
himself managed to get hold of the wrong end of the
Christian stick : in fact, I feel that he has tried to
whip Christ only to find that, like the Roman soldiers,
he was whipping a singularly unresponsive Being.
Fortunately or unfortunately we can always kill
Christ, but we can never make Him die. Without
attempting to be flippant, we may truly say that He
has a habit (many might say a bad habit) of turning
up when He is least expected.

Let us consider as carefully as possible the Shavian
attitude to Jesus Christ.

.   .   .   .   .   .

Shaw starts his investigation of the Jesus question
by worrying himself somewhat about the apparent
uniqueness of Christ. One or two other people have

also worried about this question. One or two more will until the last day hoves in sight. Shaw is not at all helpful in the matter. He merely says with, I think, a rather poor disregard of the historical background that preceded the Christian era, that, for some reason or other, Christ has been picked out by popular imagination as the Christ. Now it is obviously impossible here to do more than touch upon the problems such as the indication of Christianity in the Old Testament or the probable embryonic Christian murmur in Greek philosophy, or even the feeling of negativism in the old secular and heathen world which can imply the positive need of the Christ at the particular era in which He happened to come. I do not say that any of these backgrounds explain entirely or even satisfactorily the reason why history has hailed Christ as the Christ. But I do say that Shaw might have mentioned these things instead of suggesting that a number of great historical figures have stood in a row, while mankind (for some quite inconceivable reason) has picked Christ out and told the remainder to form fours and march away. What thinkers like Shaw never seem quite able to do is to draw the line between making the uniqueness of Christ due to some kind of indefinable and universal suggestion, and attributing this unique position as being the result of an entirely logical sequence of historical events. Shaw, obviously impressed by the mystery of the choosing by mankind of Christ to occupy a place in history held by no one else, discards the signs of the pre-Christian times and puts the whole thing down to some unexplainable, universal impulse

which has pulsated the minds of countless succeeding
generations.   Thus Shaw writes, trying to answer his
question, Why Jesus more than another ?

> " But for some reason the imagination of white
> mankind has picked out Jesus of Nazareth as *the*
> Christ and attributed all the Christian doctrines
> to Him ; and as it is the doctrine and not the
> man that matters, and, as, besides, one symbol
> is as good as another provided everyone attaches
> the same meaning to it, I raise, for the moment,
> no question as to how far the Gospels are original,
> and how far they consist of Greek and Chinese
> interpolations."

Let us, then, for the time being, leave Shaw to
puzzle out the reason why Christ has been chosen by
mankind instead of, say, Plato, Socrates, or Napoleon.
The only answer is that, of course, He happened to
choose Himself, but it is not a particularly satisfactory
one.   So we may turn to two questions that Shaw
asks—the one whether Jesus was a coward, the other
whether He was a martyr.

Bernard Shaw does get at the root of the problem
as to whether Jesus was a coward or not by saying
quite frankly that the question of cowardice is not
affected in the least by a person's Christological bias.
As Shaw remarks, the question of the cowardice of
Jesus is not in the least determined by whether He is
accepted as a Divine person or whether He is accepted
as a person with a delusion.   Whatever you may feel,
says Shaw, about Jesus, you are bound to admit that
He was possessed of distinct personal courage.   Thus

Shaw, defending the courage of Jesus, goes on to say with a quite remarkable lack of balance, that the saying, " ' Gentle Jesus, meek and mild ' is a snivelling modern invention with no warrant in the Gospels." I feel that the criticism that Shaw makes of this gentle attitude is not quite fair. The line of the famous hymn is not a modern snivelling invention, nor is it—as is more commonly supposed—a kind of sop to children. What, in my opinion, the line really does represent, is the logical character of Christ, Who could be, when it was necessary, quite gentle ; and also, when it was necessary, quite uncompromisingly stern. Somehow Shaw is falling very nearly, if not quite, into the trap that closed with such horrible effectiveness and drove Nietzsche into a madhouse— the position that implies that because Jesus was meek (a subtle form of extreme strength) He was the type of person who would gradually bring forth a system which would prove to be nothing more than a contemptible lying down under any kind of tyranny. And even is Shaw so superficial here that he goes on to suggest, with one of those deplorable sneers which have made him appear so much less valuable than he really is, that the gentle Jesus type is echoed in our modern life by the type of English curate who is manly enough to play croquet with a hard ball. Such a position is not only unworthy of Shaw but is unworthy of any professing thinker, for there is not the smallest connection between a certain clerical effeminacy which unfortunately does exist and the meekness of which Jesus was, when the occasion warranted it, the supreme example. And, apart from the fact that Shaw has grossly muddled up effeminacy and weakness, there is no question that the life of the priest is the most courageous form of life and certainly the life that is the most worth while. It is even more worth while than the worldly worthwhileness which would not drive the money-changers out of the temple but invite them to a round table conference in the city and cheat them if possible.

Let us turn then for a moment to the other question as to whether Jesus was a martyr. Bernard Shaw cannot see that He was. I agree with him. It was the followers of Jesus who were the martyrs, not Jesus Himself. Shaw now goes on to discuss the responsibility of the High Priest for indicting Jesus and looking upon Him as nothing less than a vulgar blasphemer. We are always inclined to look upon those who had the conduct of the Jesus case as criminals who condemned a man who ought to have been acquitted. Let us look at the Jesus case without any prejudice that He was God or that Pilate and his colleagues knew that the man who stood before them was going to be what He is for the orthodox—the sum of all knowledge. What was it that Caiaphas and Annas and Pilate beheld? Something, says Shaw in effect, that can be seen any morning in a lunatic asylum, that is, the really melancholy spectacle of a man possessed by a delusion. The colleagues of Pilate saw Jesus uttering a horrid and dangerous blasphemy. Without any apology whatever, with extreme tenacity, Jesus asserted that He was God. It is a little curious in passing to note that Shaw says Jesus was " executed by the Jews for the blasphemy of claiming to be a God." Nothing could be more unscholarly than such an assertion : Jesus did not claim to be a God ; He did not claim to be the God ; He claimed to be God. Let us return to the Jesus case. The principal point of interest, really, that Shaw makes in regard to it is that he warns us not to condemn those who condemned Jesus just because most of the Western nations, at any rate, have agreed that the claims of Jesus were accurate. No, let us be fair. Those who tried Jesus felt they were up against someone who might endanger the integrity of the state and someone who might smash up the Jewish religion. Here was an impertinent and impudent blasphemer claiming to be God. He must be got rid of quickly, before He did any damage. I can never understand those who belong to the orthodox church condemning the condemners of Jesus as bad men : they did their duty fearlessly, which is more than a good many Christians do to-day. Perhaps the worst charge that can be brought against Caiaphas, Annas, and Pilate is that they suffered from a lack of imagination. They could not see (I refuse to concede that they *would* not see) that when they lifted up Christ on the Cross they would never be able to take Him down. Had they said, Well, if you are God, do your worst about it, we might never have heard of Christ again. And I emphasise that I am assuming that the judges of Jesus were correct in thinking that He suffered from a delusion that was blasphemous. If it is true that Christ is God, then there is not the smallest interest in the story, for the whole thing is pre-arranged and inevitable, and Caiaphas,

Annas, and Pilate were simply pawns in the divine game.

And Shaw demands that the modern world would treat Jesus as a madman and send Him to a lunatic asylum, whereas the High Priest treated Him as a blasphemer because he was looking forward to the coming of the Messiah.

We now arrive at the really important part of the Shavian discussion on the question of Christ. How far does Shaw go with Jesus Christ? He likes the circumstances of His birth as narrated by St. Luke ; he considers St. Luke a fine literary artist who can describe with great charm the picturesque events which lead up to Mary crowded out of the inn and finding refuge in a stable. He is intrigued by the subtle way in which St. Luke narrates the romantic mystery of the whole affair by telling us that the momentous events in the stable not only drew the wise kings from the East, but re-echoed up to Heaven so that the heavenly hosts pilgrimaged to earth. · He sees St. Luke the master man of letters who is not content to let the Annunciation be made to Joseph but invests it with charm, so that the Holy Ghost addresses Mary herself. So far, indeed, does Shaw go in his intense admiration of St. Luke that he infers that Luke has painted such a glowing picture of Christ that it is the Lukan Christ who has captured the world's imagination, whereas the Christ of St. Matthew was a rather hard and unpleasant figure. It is impossible, of course, here even to touch on the Synoptic problem, that the gospels, with the exception of the fourth Gospel, have a common origin. And, after all, we should probably find that if three men wrote about one man we should get, not three characters, but one man shown to us with so much of his character that it might quite conceivably look like three characters. Undoubtedly St. Luke wrote extraordinarily well, but he had, perhaps, the easiest gospel to write. Thus does Shaw praise so highly the third Gospel, suggesting with, I think, inaccuracy, that at least part of its intention was to be an antidote to the less ornate Gospel attributed to St. Matthew.

> " In short, every device is used to get rid of the ruthless horror of the Matthew chronicle, and to relieve the strain of the Passion by touching episodes, and by representing Christ as superior to human suffering. It is Luke's Jesus who has won our hearts."

The fourth Gospel, the battle-ground of the New Testament, surprises Shaw. Shaw sees in the Johannine Christ a more intricate Being than the Christ of the Synoptic Gospels. It is again impossible here to go into the question at all, but it needs but a careful reading to discover that the Figure described in the first three Gospels is every bit as intricate as that described in the fourth. Shaw sees the Christ of the fourth Gospel a much more assertive Figure than that shown by the other Gospels. He argues much more, is irritated by the dislike of the Jews, is earnestly concerned with the worth of His own Resurrection, and causes a popular outburst of dislike by His suggestion that His body must be eaten. And Shaw remarks that He says many apparently

contradictory and nonsensical things. But perhaps
they are only nonsensical when taken away from their
context. In a word, Shaw finds the Figure in the
fourth Gospel a sophisticated Mystic. As long, then,
as Christ stands out as a great human Figure Shaw is
not particularly upset about it. But then all at once
there is a sudden and startling change. And it is a
change for the worse. St. Peter, always the most
impetuous of the disciples, suddenly literally shouts
with all the enthusiasm of a man who has solved a
great problem, " Thou art the Christ, the son of the
living God."

We are now on the horns of a pleasing little
dilemma. Is St. Peter merely carried away by hero
worship, or, for the very good reason that he is to
found the Church, is a special revelation given to
him ? There does not seem to be any decided answer
to the question, except to those who accept the
Divinity of Christ in its entirety. What is the result
that Shaw sees by this profound declaration by St.
Peter ? One thing, at any rate, is quite obvious.
Jesus accepts the Petrine homage with intense
pleasure. As Shaw says, He is pleased and excited.
Perhaps for the moment Jesus is almost like a clergyman who finds on his breakfast table a letter which
contains the offer of a bishopric. He is pleased that
St. Peter has discovered who He really is. He praises
St. Peter, makes an amusing pun of his name, and
tells him that he will be the leader on whom the
Church will be founded. Thus is the effect that Shaw
sees made on Jesus by St. Peter. But here Shaw
parts company with the orthodox Christians. Jesus

accepts St. Peter's declaration because He is under the delusion that He is God. He is delighted to find the delusion accepted : He becomes possessed of a fixed idea ; He chatters about it to His disciples with all the energy that a man spends when he is a great hero among a small band of people. Shaw sees that not only has the Petrine declaration confirmed the divinity delusion of Jesus, but it alters His character. He becomes arrogant, dictatorial, and even abusive. And Shaw is rather upset when the fig tree is cursed for bearing no fruit. Thus Shaw sees Jesus keeping His delusion and finally dying on the cross.

After three days the Resurrection takes place and Shaw writes the amazing truth, "The story has no ending."

.   .   .   .   .

We may as well now turn to a further consideration concerning the character of Jesus. Shaw discusses Him as an Economist and as a Biologist.

We are now, of course, dealing with the utilitarian value of Jesus in modern life. And in dealing with Jesus as an economist, Shaw is perfectly right in saying it did not matter whether He was God or not. In Shaw's eyes Jesus was an excellent economist because he taught the eternal truth that we need not worry about the next day. And, as Shaw points out, He taught that we should be gentlemen instead of commercialised cads. And no country is more full of these people than England. We worship money because we love false gods. We invite money-grubbers to take food with us instead of allowing them to feed in the pigsty.   Only too truly, as Shaw points out, did Jesus emphasise that where our treasure is there shall be found our heart as well.   And our treasure is money and it has utterly destroyed the heart.   And we do, as Shaw points out, sell our souls and bodies by the pound and the inch after wasting half the day in haggling over the price.   The men who teach the young that they must live for money will only learn the folly of their ways when they find that the Angel of Death is not to be bribed by money, nor is he in the least impressed by the white-spatted man who passes the Mansion House.   Death is much more impressed by the despised Carpenter who smashed up the tomb, and is ever smashing up the false values that make us all such desperate failures.

In Shaw's opinion Jesus was also a first-rate biologist.   He taught that though we die like men we are all in reality gods.   Shaw does not see the biological doctrines of Jesus touched by evolution.   Perhaps Shaw is specially pleased at the biological position of Christ, for it points towards the evolution of the superman.   And we grow towards being supermen because God is Spirit.   And it is perhaps rather curious that Shaw does not see that naturally Jesus would teach of God as being a spirit because He happened to be that spirit Himself.   We cannot, says Shaw, touch the spiritual doctrine of Jesus, but we can, he asserts, smash up the theologians who have conceived God as a kind of super-magnate.   Dear Mr. Shaw, how simple he is sometimes.   Of course we can smash up such theologians, for they are merely pseudo-theologians. The God who wandered about the family Bible in white robes may have gone, as Shaw suggests, but His spirit still sings out from the high hills of God, " Lo, I am with you always, even unto the end of the world."

Let us consider briefly what Shaw has to say concerning the historical fact that Jesus did not marry. In a former book I remarked that one probable reason was that Jesus was not interested in any woman. And also that, taking the story of His life exactly as it was, his worldly position was not likely to attract any woman. I have already dealt in detail with Shaw and the question of marriage, so it is not necessary here to touch on the more general discussion concerning Jesus and Marriage and the Family. We must ask why it was, in Shaw's opinion, Jesus did not marry. He has no sympathy with those who " regard Him as a god descended from His throne in heaven to take on humanity " and " declare that the assumption of humanity must have been incomplete at its most vital point if He were a celibate." The very reverse of this is much more pleasing to Shaw. He sees only too truly that to many people the mere thought of Jesus being married is simply a blasphemous suggestion. The real reason quite obviously why Jesus did not marry was that He had a great deal too much work to do to be able to be hampered by any home ties. Shaw writes fully understanding the non-marrying position.

" It is evident from His impatience when people excused themselves from following Him because of their family funerals, or when they assumed that His first duty was to His mother, that He had found family ties and domestic affection in His way at every turn, and had become persuaded at last that no man could follow His inner light until He was free from their compulsion."

It is perhaps a convenient place in which to turn to something of what Shaw says about the apostles. They are for Shaw the arch offenders, they have dragged down Christianity and made it into a complicated system. Most untruly and most unfairly he writes :

" He was hardly cold in his grave, or high in His heaven (as you please), before the apostles dragged the tradition of Him down to the level of the thing it has remained ever since."

It is untrue to write thus, and merely shows a failure even to think about any of the really intricate sayings of Christ. It is absurd to accuse St. Paul of complicating Christian doctrine when the whole of Christianity is one long complication. Because the usual mass of church people do not understand St. Paul is no good reason for accusing him of inventing doctrines that were never suggested by Jesus. Who could enunciate a more complicated statement than He Who declared that He was the Logos, that He would rise again on the third day, that He would die on the Cross and that the Cross should be a magnet to the whole world ?

BERNARD SHAW AND CHRISTIANITY 149

Like all thinkers of the type of Shaw who are incessantly shouting for the simple Jesus of the Gospels and declaring that the apostles have turned the simple utterances of Jesus into a profound system, Shaw makes an attack on St. Paul. Thus he writes in this way : " There is not one word of Pauline Christianity in the characteristic utterances of Jesus." Of course there is not: there is no such thing as Pauline Christianity. There is the Christianity that St. Paul taught; simply the Christianity that Christ revealed to St. Paul and allowed him to teach. To suggest that St. Paul invented his own Christianity is entirely to misinterpret the whole nature of the New Testament. It is also safe to say that there is not one word of Pauline Christianity which cannot be inferred in the characteristic utterances of Jesus. The attack that Shaw makes on St. Paul is quite unmerited.

The influence of St. Paul will exist to the end of time and, of course, the attack, like all attacks on St. Paul, merely strengthens him. But it is a pity that Shaw now and again wastes his extraordinary talent by dealing with matters about which he really seems to know very little. Any scholar can prove over and over again that St. Paul in no sense added to the Christian doctrine, but simply explained it. There is no opposition whatever between Jesus and Paul : Jesus was the leader and Paul followed and did what he was told. Shaw has missed the point entirely here in thinking that St. Paul complicated Christian doctrine. He simply states it, and it had to be explained in language that would be

understood by the people to whom it was explained.
Let us leave the matter here and follow Shaw when
he deals with some other aspects of Christianity.

·   ·   ·   ·   ·

Bernard Shaw deals very skilfully with what he
calls the peril of the Iconoclast.   What he sees is that
you may attack Jesus on many grounds and be considered a mere intellectualist, but if you dare to
suggest that He was a real person in the sense of
having any kind of a weakness, you are at once
accused of blasphemy.   As Shaw points out you may
perfectly easily deny the divinity of Christ and be
nothing more than a pleasant kind of agnostic, but
should you make any remarks about the personal
appearance of Christ, you are at once uttering a
dangerous and disgusting blasphemy.   Shaw puts the
matter a little crudely but undoubtedly with a great
deal of common-sense.   For he writes :

> " You may deny the divinity of Jesus ; you
> may doubt whether he ever existed ; you may
> reject Christianity for Judaism, Mohammedanism,
> Shintoism, or Fire Worship ; and the icono-
> clasters, placidly contemptuous, will only classify
> you as a freethinker or a heathen.   But if you
> venture to wonder how Christ would have looked
> if he had shaved and had his hair cut, or what
> size in shoes he took, or whether he swore when
> he stood on a nail in the carpenter's shop, or
> could not button his robe when he was in a
> hurry, or whether he laughed over the repartees
> by which he baffled the priests when they tried

to trap him into sedition and blasphemy, or even
if you tell any part of his story in the vivid
terms of modern colloquial slang, you will
produce an extraordinary dismay and horror
among the iconoclasters."

Now there are two kinds of thinkers who would
conceive of Christ in this way and be really interested
in knowing whether He shaved or not for two distinct
reasons. The one set of thinkers would want to
stress the humanity of Christ so that they could feel
He was a more reasonable leader than the mystic
figure adopted by the Church. The other set of
thinkers would wish to stress the humanity of Christ
because they would feel that if He really was real they
would be up against something quite terrifying. It
does not need much imagination to conceive of the
remarkable change that would come over society were
society really to believe in Christ. If Christ could
to-day be proved to be a really live person we should
find all our values changed with a most uncomfortable
speed. It would be a most terrible bore to the large
number of people who recite the command to love
their neighbours as themselves to find that the
originator of the command was as much alive as
Ramsay Macdonald. As Bernard Shaw points cut
with delightful irony, the one thing society must not
do if it is going to live is to bring Christ to life. It
might even upset the pious in the Church, which
would be terribly disturbing for them. We might
find our bishops told to clear out of their palaces and
embrace the itinerant poverty that always embraced

L

Christ. We might find the mobs of high-born ladies
kneeling before the altar told that continuous genu-
flecting in front of the High Altar was not a substitute
for tyranny in the domestic kitchen. Thus Shaw
writes with a grim irony warning the Christians of the
terrible things that will happen to them, should the
fact be revealed that Christ is act ially *not* dead :

> " The moment it strikes you (as it may any
> day) that Christ is not the lifeless, harmless
> image he has hitherto been to you, but a rallying
> centre for revolutionary influences which all
> established States and Churches fight, you must
> look to yourselves ; for you have brought the
> image to life ; and the mob may not be able to
> bear that horror."

Immediately after this warning Shaw proceeds to
consider the War in relation to Christianity. We are
all aware that the War was a terrible reminder of our
failure to make Christianity a living force. Christianity
did not fail because of the War : Christianity failed
because we had never yet tried it. So Shaw writes :
" It did not need the present War to show that
neither the iconographic Christ nor the Christ of St.
Paul has succeeded in effecting the salvation of human
society." Shaw will insist that there are several
manufactured Christs, and unless one has a firm
critical background the error is easy enough to fall
into. However, Shaw writes a terrible indictment of
the dreadful way in which the Western World has
either been content with a dead Christ or no Christ
at all. For he tells us the terrible truth that we who

profess to be Christians cannot logically complain of non-Christian practices, however abominable, because, as the War proved, we are merely Christian in name and heathen in practice. He points out, only too truly, that we cannot even express disgust that the Turks massacre the Armenians, for we, with all our churches and priests and bishops, with all our daily feedings on the Body and Blood of Christ, concentrated all our energies on massacring the Germans with much less excuse than the Turks had for their reprehensible conduct. I am afraid it is only too true, as Shaw says, that at present Barabbas is triumphant everywhere : his triumph is even not without triumph in the Church. Our clergy fight for high offices : our politicians find the making of armaments more necessary than the making of Christians : our cities are so foul that they are founded on lust and lies. But, as Shaw points out, there is a remedy. And, as he puts it, rather crudely, the remedy for all these things may lie in the fact that Jesus is not such a fool as He is thought and that all our boasted civilisation is not much good, unless it sometimes thinks back to the night when events of considerable importance happened in an obscure Eastern stable.

Let us consider somewhat further what Shaw thinks is the practical use of the teachings of Jesus in modern life.

Shaw does deal extraordinarily well with the difficulties of applying the precepts of Jesus to modern conditions. The difficulty, of course, is not the application of the Jesus ethics to modern life, but the reshuffling of modern life so that it will reasonably

attune itself to the Jesus sayings. Or rather, we
should have to make universal that which Dean
Inge calls so aptly " the transvaluation of values."
Bernard Shaw takes as a quite excellent example
what we might expect if we asked a modern stockbroker to act simply as Jesus advised his disciples to
act. The reply we shall get, Shaw tells us, is : " You
are advising me to become a tramp." Now it is, of
course, a possibility that the tramp lives a more real
life than the stockbroker. That is not the point.
Supposing it be admitted that Jesus would ask a
modern stockbroker to act as the disciples—would it
not be that He would ask him to act in the spirit of
the disciples ? If we are firmly convinced that Jesus
was no fool (as Shaw admits), then surely He would
not ask a man to become a stockbroker and immediately ask him to behave in such a fashion that he
would become at once a non-stockbroker, in other
words, a tramp. What, of course, we might expect
Jesus to say is—you can be a Christian stockbroker,
when the phrase means something more than mere
honourable business on weekdays and a round of golf
on Sundays—you can make it so that were I to
arrive suddenly in London I could pick out any twelve
stockbrokers and make them just as efficient disciples
as the various people I collected into my original
twelve on the shores of Galilee !

Shaw complains of a Christian precept which, he
feels, though good enough an ideal, is unpractical.
He says truly enough that it is impossible for the
rich man to sell all that he has and give it to the poor.
Why is it impossible ? Because, says Shaw only too

truly, the poor man will not be helped. The rich man in London sells ten thousand pounds' worth of property. The man who buys it must be a rich man. The poor will not get any benefit by the exchange of property. There is surely a danger in taking all these sayings of a sociological nature too literally. Surely the implication in the Jesus precept, " Sell all and give to the poor," is simply an implication that a man must be ready at any cost to help his neighbour. I mean, if you take the saying that a rich man must sell his goods and give to the poor quite literally, it is a little difficult also to take literally the saying that the poor are always with us. For it will simply mean a vicious circle leaving with us everlastingly the rich who are willing to give and the poor who are willing to receive. It is all very well for Shaw to cry out furiously against poverty. The fact does remain that from the point of view of Christianity, poverty does not seem to be a crime, and Shaw does view poverty as something criminal, in the sense that it is a crime inducer. Again, he says rather airily that the distribution of wealth is all wrong. He cries out angrily : " We have million-dollar babies side by side with paupers worn out by a long life of unremitted drudgery." But the evil does not lie in the parallel lines of great wealth and great poverty, but the evil comes when the million-dollar baby is brought up to have no interest at all in the baby that has only two dollars. Surely the whole question of the distribution of wealth is summed up by the great command which rather upset the disciples—we must love (and I feel the Greek word might quite well imply an economic care of our neighbour) our neighbour as ourselves.

Shaw deals very interestingly with the problem of crime and punishment. He tells us that what Jesus meant with regard to justice is that it was foolish to adopt punishment and call it justice. So Shaw writes showing up the anomaly of our system of so-called justice by which the judge reduces himself to the level of the criminal. Our judges are, of course, not the symbol of justice but the symbol of the abominable failure of our social system. We have no right to send any one to prison, because we have made the criminals. We have no right to hang a murderer, because we make all murderers. The judge who administers punishment under the pretence of justice is a despicable criminal. The magistrate in the country town who administers justice should be hounded out of the place as a hypocrite and liar. So Shaw writes his explanation of why Jesus said " Judge not that ye be not judged."

> " People without self-control enough for social purposes may be killed, or may be kept in asylums with a view to studying their condition and ascertaining whether it is curable. To torture them and give ourselves virtuous airs at their expense is ridiculous and barbarous ; and the desire to do it is vindictive and cruel. And though vindictiveness and cruelty are at least human qualities when they are frankly proclaimed and indulged, they are loathsome when they assume the robes of Justice. Which, I take it, is why Shakespeare's Isabella gave such a

dressing-down to Judge Angelo, and why Swift
reserved the hottest corner of his hell for judges.
Also, of course, why Jesus said ' Judge not that
ye be not judged ' and ' If any man hear my
words and believe not, I judge him not ' because
' he hath one that judgeth him ' : namely, the
Father who is one with Him."

And as though to prove his contention that to call
punishment the ally of justice is to be guilty of
beastly hypocrisy, Shaw asks pertinently enough
what economical good has been achieved by disobeying all through the centuries the Jesus precept, Judge
not ? Shaw challenges anyone to show that from any
point of view the world has been any better than if
there had never been a judge, a prison, or a gallows
at all. There is no answer, for we cannot give a ver-
dict on history that has not existed. But if Jesus
was God and therefore infallible, we have obviously
made a mistake in disobeying His injunction.

I have dealt with a few aspects of Shaw's attitude
to Jesus and Christianity. It will therefore be as well
to say a little about the methods he would like to see
adopted for the teaching of Christianity. Shaw
wishes to see children delivered from a number of
proselytisers with the proselytising atheist at one end
and the proselytising nun at the other. The proselytising atheist should certainly be incarcerated in a
lunatic asylum ; to make any kind of attack on nuns
is quite beside the point. Shaw is very insistent that
we must not worry children with idle controversies as
to whether there was ever such a person as Jesus or

not. He puts the matter very excellently when he
writes thus :

> "We must cut the controversy short by
> declaring that there is the same evidence for the
> existence of Jesus as for that of any other person
> of his time ; and the fact that you may not
> believe everything Matthew tells you no more
> disproves the existence of Jesus than the fact
> that you do not believe everything Macaulay
> tells you disproves the existence of William III."

The leading up to the DEEPER Christianity must be,
Shaw feels, a very gradual process. It is enough at
first to know that history authenticates the existence
of the historical Jesus. The doctrines then can be
added and considered as psychological phenomena.
The child can then accept them as he likes. There is,
of course, the objection that the acceptance of a faith
is something more than the expression of a wish. But
that is as far as Bernard Shaw goes. He puts his
position perfectly simply.

> "Then, as the child's mind matures, it can
> learn, as historical and psychological phenomena,
> the tradition of the scapegoat, the Redeemer,
> the Second Coming, and how, in a world saturated
> with this tradition, Jesus has been largely
> accepted as the long-expected and often proph-
> esied Redeemer, the Messiah, THE Christ. It is
> open to the child to accept him."

And Shaw then enunciates the rather precarious
proposition, that the question of acceptance will
depend on the temperament of the child. This, of

course, leaves on one side something that might be
called the impelling necessity of believing in Christianity. It leaves on one side the possibility that we may
have to accept the Christian creed whether we like it
or not. Shaw also forgets that you cannot learn of
the Resurrection, the Second Coming, and then just
throw them over without feeling some sense of loss,
which may (and often does) lead to permanent disappointment and delusion. There is a good deal to
be said for Shaw's suggestions, and a good deal more
to be said against them.

. . . . .

Shaw arrives at the end of the Jesus discussion with
the following conclusion :

" Jesus certainly did not consider the overthrow of the Roman Empire or the substitution
of a new ecclesiastical organisation for the Jewish
Church or for the priesthood of the Roman gods
as part of his programme."

The Shavian discussion is valuable in so far as
any discussion by a clear thinker is valuable. Now
and again Shaw has something new to say about
Jesus : now and again he would be considered
irreverent, but such a criticism would mistake
language for spirit. Shaw takes the Jesus question
as an historical question : he looks at it from many
sides : he goes into the problem of the practicability
of Christianity to our modern life. Perhaps the most
striking thought that he has is that civilisation will
come down with a horrid bump when it discovers that

Jesus is a real and live person.   Shaw, as I have tried
to point out, deals quite unfairly with St. Paul.   In
doing this he merely falls in line with those thinkers
who find the utterances so simple because they never
study them.   St. Paul may have said one or two
involved things about Christ : Christ said more than
one or two about Himself.

The first Christmas night may have beheld a small
Baby who cried for His mother.   The last Christmas
night will behold the same small Baby very much
grown up and enunciating so that all those who have
ever lived and died shall listen.   For He will say on
the last Christmas day from the top of the mountain
that can be seen by all peoples :

> " I am the first and the last, and the living
> one ; and I was dead, and behold, I am alive for
> ever more, and I have the keys of death and of
> Hades."

PART IV

SHAW AND THE SALVATION ARMY

SHAW AND CHILDREN

SAINT JOAN

BERNARD SHAW TO-DAY AND TO-MORROW

Chapter I

SHAW AND THE SALVATION ARMY

IN his preface to *Major Barbara*, Shaw indulges in a characteristic grumble. Once again his critics do not give him credit for the powers of originality that he possesses. This, then, is the particular Shavian grumble. Shaw complains that whenever he writes anything that might puzzle the mentality of a church-warden, the professional critics, who are, after all, mostly journalists, turn round and praise Shaw and then naïvely suggest that, excellent as his art is, it must of course be dependent upon Schopenhauer, Nietzsche, Ibsen, Strindberg, Tolstoy, or some other excellent gentleman who might be found drinking coffee or beer in some European capital. The grumble has, I think, a certain amount of merit. We are quite inclined to think that English or Irish art or, for that matter, Scotch or Welsh art, cannot be expected to be violently original. We admit freely enough that Great Britain can produce work that is expression of genius, but we are disposed to conclude that it is in a sense " copyist " genius. It is probably true that European drama, with the exception of Shakespeare, has a greater degree of originality than English drama. The reason is not far to seek. European drama consists of totally different kinds of dramatists from totally different kinds of countries.

The national point of view of drama is different in almost every country. Norway—cold ; Russia— cruel and whimsical ; Germany—inclined to domesticity.   But I do not wish to be misunderstood when I say that, to a certain extent, the outlook of English drama is at a certain level.   When, then, the professional critics (many of whom simply see the drama they are paid to see) are nonplussed at Shaw's originality and therefore suspect foreign influences, we can hardly blame them, seeing that the average Englishman thinks it improbable, if not impossible, to find a British dramatist completely original off his own bat.

The particular reason why Shaw starts his preface to *Major Barbara* with the grumble I have mentioned here is that he is courteous enough to put before the critics his reason for telling them in advance what they ought to say about his play.   *Major Barbara* is an extremely true picture of the point of view of the Salvation Army.   The Salvation Army is undoubtedly something of a nuisance when it disturbs multitudes of mechanical citizens on a Sunday morning.   It is a little irritating to them when they have been cheating their neighbours all the week to be suddenly reminded rather discordantly on Sunday morning that salvation does not lie that way.   The Salvation Army is a disturbing influence.   It is, fortunately, not nearly so well-mannered as the Church of England, and has a no doubt vastly reprehensible habit of taking religion, the shouting kind of religion, to the homes of the citizens.

The plot behind *Major Barbara* is not important as a plot but it is important as picking up, as it were, into a kernel, a sociological problem that, like most sociological problems, is abominably unpleasant because it affects all of us, whether it is our fault or not. The plot then, or the theme rather, behind *Major Barbara* is the simple fact that the Salvation Army is kept going by finance which comes from sources which it is out to destroy. Here, then, we may expect to find Shaw enjoying himself immensely. The whole affair is pretty disturbing and Shaw has no intention of letting us off. We most of us sympathise with the young clergyman who starts his life with a pious intention of saving people who would be bored to distraction by such a process ; we all sympathise with him as he struggles to be intellectual without daring to proceed beyond certain set boundaries of intellectualism. We sympathise with him when his generous parishioners pay him sufficient for him to have a clean shirt every Sunday, but—and here comes in the Shavian two-edged sword—we seldom, if ever, sympathise with the young clergyman because he is bound to accept money from hypocritical scoundrels or die and relegate his spiritual mission to someone else. Shaw does see the zealous young clergyman getting a very nasty quarter of an hour when he is so unwise as to probe down into the source of his income. For what does he discover ? Merely this. That he is the servant not only of God but of many of the forces against God. More likely than not the main subscriber to his quarterly stipend is the local brewer— a very charming personality who goes to church on Sunday and helps to undo the work of the Church every other day. The Church fights against drink,

the abominable evil that fills the homes of the poor
with squalor and misery, the abominable evil that
fills the lunatic asylums with dehumanised beings
who must be secluded from human vision, the abominable evil which turns the side streets of a city like
London or Manchester on a Saturday night into a
cesspool.

Let us follow the poor young clergyman a little
further. Everything is not so cut and dried as it
seemed at the theological college. The Church has
worse evils to fight than Arianism, Sabellianism, or
even Ecclesiasticism. In a moment of spiritual
abandon he will decide to refrain from taking any
more money from the prosperous and generous brewer :
he will give up his curacy : he will drag his unfortunate
wife to a new experience of being weighed up by her
husband's new congregation: he will determine that
his stipend shall only come from the old ladies who
are ever his most ardent supporters. Even so he has
not solved his problem. He soon discovers that the
old ladies get their incomes from manufacturers who
encourage prostitution by the employment of cheap
female labour. So there is the conclusion that the
unfortunate young clergyman must either acquiesce
in the financial methods of the Church or give up his
job altogether. The problem is not exaggerated.
Almost every, if not every, institution is supported by
money derived from sources against which it is pledged
to fight. In Shaw's play dealing with the Salvation
Army, the particular problem is whether a particular
branch of the Salvation Army shall accept a sum of
money from a manufacturer of munitions. Shaw,

while distressed at the fact that religious bodies are forced to derive their income from people whose daily occupation is anti-religious, does not in one direction go far enough. He rightly sees the anomaly of the money of a brewer helping on the work of the Church ; he rightly sees that the Church must set its face against drink. But he does not seem to see that what the Church really must set her face against is not drink but the abuse of it. The evil of most brewers is not that they are brewers, but that the more drunkenness there is, the better they are pleased. The more drunkenness, the more servants they can have : the more drunkenness, the more hunters they can keep : the more drunkenness, the more subscriptions they can give to hospitals and churches.

This preliminary Shavian indictment of the source of income that supports religious bodies as a whole, and the Salvation Army in particular, leads in to a side issue which it is as well to consider here, before turning back to a further discussion of Shaw's attitude to the Salvation Army. The main disturbing influence in *Major Barbara* is, of course, Andrew Undershaft. We might really make a pun on his name and say that the whole trouble about him is that he never intended to be an underdog. The problem of Undershaft leads to the Shavian *bête noir*—the crime, as he calls it, of poverty. And the Salvation Army are fundamentally the fighters not only against their own poverty but against the appalling criminal poverty which makes their fight so inevitable. Every country that boasts of a civilisation that drives mankind into great towns produces a series of cesspools.

M

Undershaft is one of the most typical of the Shavian characters.   He is a man possessed of something that can only be described as evil genius.   Two paths lie open to him : he can follow the dictates of his evil genius and become (as he does become) a manufacturer of munitions and a gentleman of wealth ; he can leave his evil genius on one side and lead the life of a poor man.   Now, at first sight, it would seem that the choice is merely the difficult choice that probably comes to more people than we imagine, the choice not between good and evil but the choice between a life of perpetual subordination to intellectual inferiors, or the attainment of wealth and position by creative work that is paradoxically destructive.   " Hobson's Choice," if you like, but that is not the choice that Shaw sees.   Undershaft is not called upon to choose between something that had better perhaps be called good or evil, but he has to choose between energetic enterprise or the kind of subtle cowardice which is really the attribute of all who choose a subordinate job in preference to assuming the responsibilities of a creator or leader.   Shaw does see that, had Undershaft refused to exercise his talent which led him to be the head of a huge munition factory, he would really be in danger of disobeying the very Gospel itself.   It would be straying beyond our subject to discuss the dreadful problem that Undershaft does present, that many of us do seem to have entirely destructive talent, and yet to ignore these talents is to ignore entirely the divine energy implanted within us.   Here, then, in Shaw's own words, is Undershaft's position :

" Undershaft, the hero of *Major Barbara*, is simply a man who, having grasped the fact that poverty is a crime, knows that when society offered him the alternative of poverty or a lucrative trade in death or destruction, it offered him, not a choice between opulent villainy and humble virtue, but between energetic enterprise and cowardly infamy."

Wealth, to Undershaft, is not a matter of gain, but a matter of honour.   So Shaw's standpoint.   For what, he asks, does poverty do ?   It means that a man is weak, that he will remain without knowledge, that he will live in dirt, think in dirt, become mentally dirty, dull, torpid, unable to assert himself, the prey of conditions that he dare not protest against, cowardly, dragging up his children in an atmosphere so that when he dies they will scream at his coffin that it contains the criminal who has left behind the very doubtful benefit of an unsmirched name.   Poverty, so Shaw goes on in his indictment of it, will encourage cheap labour, will infect our cities with whole neighbourhoods of poisonous slums, will make our streets mere parades in which rich men and rich women will push the poor unceremoniously out of the way.   Shaw goes so far even as to ask this question, such is his violent hatred of poverty :

" Would he not (the poor man) do ten times less harm as a prosperous burglar, incendiary, ravisher, or murderer, to the utmost limits of humanity's comparatively negligible impulses in these directions ? "

This is, of course, Shaw gaining our interest by a somewhat exaggerated supposition. What, he demands, would be the sensible method of crucifying poverty so that the third day should see it still well in the tomb of popular abandonment, would be " to give every man enough to live well on, so as to guarantee the community against the possibility of a case of the malignant disease of poverty, and then (necessarily) to see that he earned it."

Let us turn back to a more definite consideration of the Salvation Army itself. Whether or not Shaw attacks or defends the Salvation Army, *Major Barbara* contains many extremely sensible and, I should imagine, accurate, pictures of the mentality of Salvation Army officials and those they have to deal with.

Although Shaw is always contemptuous of the professional soldier, he agrees at once that the title " Salvation Army " is peculiarly appropriate. For the essence of the designation is that salvation cannot be obtained merely by prayer, but must be obtained by a kind of disciplinary offensive action against the devil. There is a remarkable dipping back into history in the comparatively modern creation of the Salvation Army. The whole of the Old Testament, taken as a progressive didactic philosophy, and not as a series of isolated man to God or God to man movements, is a kind of rather cheery marshalling of forces, with almost a kind of military precision, against the enemies of Jehovah.

Thus Shaw writes about the significance of the title Salvation Army :

" Does it not suggest that the Salvationists divine that they must actually fight the devil instead of merely praying at him ? At present, it is true, they have not quite ascertained his correct address. When they do, they may give a very rude shock to that sense of security which he has gained from his experience of the fact that hard words, even when uttered by eloquent essayists and lecturers, or carried unanimously at enthusiastic public meetings on the motion of eminent reformers, break no bones."

In spite of certain weaknesses in the Salvation Army which Shaw discovers, and which I shall consider here, he finds the Salvation Army in essence something that can legitimately produce optimism. He finds the Salvation Army quite capable of asserting its mission to a hostile world. It can even be unflattered by the friendly or unfriendly attention of rich idlers amusing themselves by looking on at some fancy religion. He discerns it a preaching body but not a body that preaches submission to all the evils that are passed because they look respectable. It is quite oblivious to abuse for the simple reason that the more successful it is the more it will become abused. Abuse not from sinners but from complacent saints. It is not afraid to proclaim the good news in a cheery, music-hall fashion, instead of announcing it as though the good news had to be proclaimed with long faces. The world, so Shaw sees, will find the Salvation Army a menace because the Salvation Army implies hope. Hope, the birthright of the poor, the one thing the

rich must never let them have if possible. We may
turn to discuss a few of the weaknesses that seem to
be embodied in the Salvation Army. Shaw points
out that it has almost as many weaknesses as the
Church of England, which is disturbing for that body.
A first and great weakness that Shaw spots is, of
course, the fact that the bigger the Salvation Army
becomes, the more must it be governed on business
lines. He scents the possibility of the Salvation Army
being governed by a bureaucracy of business men
who will be, if possible, more unscrupulous than the
bishops. I cannot understand why Shaw will continually gibe at bishops—men who are of all men
least likely to act in defiance of Shavian principles.
The bishops are much too busy to be tyrants. When
the bishops were unscrupulous they were not in the
least unscrupulous about the things that worry Shaw.
They were unscrupulous about precisely the things
that never have worried him, to wit, spiritual values
and various interpretations of doctrines. It is also
quite absurd to suppose that if the Salvation Army is
ruled by a governing body of bureaucrats that they
will also be at the same time pernicious autocrats. If
Shaw would sometimes realise that organisation does
not always mean tyranny, he would be saved making
foolish gibes at people of whom he obviously knows
nothing whatever.

Now there is a tremendous amount of truth, on
the other hand, when Shaw demands that all religious
bodies, and in particular, the Salvation Army, cannot
indulge in a vigorous revolt against riches and, says
Shaw, for the reason that rich people would cut off

supplies of money. Nothing is further from the truth. The reason that the big religious bodies cannot indulge in revolt against riches is the extremely elementary fact that they are not self-supporting. Now let us pass on to another weakness that Shaw discovers. It is, of course, something that may be defined as a weakness concerned with metaphysics. The religious bodies are always assailed on two opposite grounds by two opposing types of people. One class, which is inclined to look upon the religious bodies as sociological reforming powers, incline to the position that religion may just as well concern itself entirely with the problems of this universe. The other school of thinkers, those who would deny to the religious bodies any right to suggest our economic policy, are inclined to adopt the position that all they need be concerned with is the preparation of people for some other kind of existence, however vague and unsatisfactory it may prove to be. Bernard Shaw condemns the Salvation Army on the ground that it holds out a kind of automatic righting, in some future existence, of wrongs endured here. In a word, Shaw discovers too much other worldliness in the Salvation Army. It has—for him—an objectionable habit " of talking as if the Salvationists were heroically enduring a very bad time on earth as an investment which will bring them in dividends later on in the form, not of a better life to come for the whole world, but of an eternity spent by themselves personally in a sort of bliss which would bore any active person to a second death."

Shaw now becomes quite angry but not so angry as

he is going to be a little later.   The Salvation Army
has a nasty habit of confession.   Shaw objects to it
most strongly.   With a gross disregard of fairness or
accuracy Shaw implies that the Salvation Army
makes use of its system of confession for mere publicity
purposes.   Such a position is completely unsound.
The reason that the Salvation Army employs confession is the same reason for which it is employed
by the Catholic Church.   It is a psychological outlet.
The confessee is like a man who is seasick : he gets
rid of something and is all the better for so doing.
Confession is not only good for the soul—it is more
often than not the sole method of getting a new start.

Here, then, Shaw writes in my opinion completely
misunderstanding the motive of confession in the
Salvation Army.

> " When you advertise a converted burglar or
> reclaimed drunkard as one of the attractions at
> an experience meeting, your burglar can hardly
> have been too burglarious or your drunkard too
> drunken."

That is true, but the reason that Shaw gives is
libellously false.   The display on the public platform
of a reformed evildoer is not a gesture of publicity
but a policy of encouragement for those who think
they are too far gone to be able to get back again.
Surely Bernard Shaw does not imagine for an instant
that the Salvation Army would conform to the usual
standards of the world.   When Christ remarked to
the penitent thief that he might expect a speedy end
to his miseries, I doubt whether even Bernard Shaw

would think that it was a publicity stunt staged by
Jesus for the edification or otherwise of future
generations.

So we proceed to Shaw thoroughly angry with the
Salvation Army. And the reason for his anger is his
hatred of the Cross as the symbol of salvation. That
is a matter of opinion. To some the Cross will always
be the central superstition of Christianity (it is to
Shaw) ; to others it will be its central truth. As a
matter of fact, it is neither. It is merely the climax
of what a journalist would call quite a good " story."

Let us turn to a short consideration of the qualities
of the play, *Major Barbara* itself.

. . . . .

In some ways Barbara is one of the most interesting
of the Shavian characters. She is typical of the type
of girl who will not conform to conventional ways.
We can imagine her immersed in slums while her
sister foxhunts. We can imagine her always, in a
good-natured way, "up" against her family. A very
amusing little contretemps with her mother in the
first act of the play warns us that Barbara is a bit of
a " handful." Barbara says what she means even if
the drawing-room is inclined to blush on her account.

> BARBARA. Why don't you laugh if you want to,
> Cholly ? It's good for your inside.
> LADY BRITOMART. Barbara ; you have had the
> education of a lady. Please let your father see
> that ; and don't talk like a street girl.

Fairly early on in Act I of *Major Barbara* Shaw

deals with a very pet theory of his. He is quite as enthusiastic about it as he is about the criminality of poverty. One of the minor characters makes use of the pernicious platitude that some men are honest and some are scoundrels. To which Barbara counters with the remark that there are no scoundrels. It is very important to realise exactly what Shaw means Barbara to mean by this bold and certainly unpopular assertion. She means that there are no scoundrels who are not *made* scoundrels. Men and women are never born scoundrels ; it is we, we the arch criminals if you like, we who divert their good energies and make them do that which must be described as non-good. We it is who make the good men and the good women bad, our slums, our prisons, our sweatings, our lusts, our refusal to believe in the brotherhood of nations and the larger brotherhood of man, our inability to see that we are but fellow pilgrims on such a short journey from the cradle to the grave. Men, says Barbara, are neither good nor bad, they are just children who have strayed away from God for a little time, and ere many days are past must return whence they came. Undershaft, completely non-plussed by the assertion that there are no scoundrels, rather hesitatingly asks whether then there are not good men in, of course, contradistinction to bad ones. To which Barbara replies, a typical reply of the true religious person, who really does believe in the oneness of humanity. We can hear Shaw speaking all the time.

BARBARA. No, not one. There are neither good

men nor scoundrels : there are just children of
one Father ; and the sooner they stop calling one
another names the better. You needn't talk to
me : I know them. I've had scores of them
through my hands : scoundrels, criminals, in-
fidels, philanthropists, missionaries, county coun-
cillors, all sorts. They're all just the same sort of
sinner ; and there's the same salvation for them
all.

That is perhaps the reason of the chaplain's words
when sentence of death has been passed. No hope
from man, no hope after condemnation by the legal
murderers, nothing but the awful nights and days in
the condemned cell—but " May the Lord have mercy
on your soul." The last exit from the dock, but not
even that desperate moment is blank despair, for
there is mercy for the murderer, for they are " just
children of one Father."

Lady Britomart is the type of person who, while
making Shaw angry, amuses him at the same time.
She is quite outrageously conventional. She can be
found in any English country town, doing good works
and boring everybody by so doing. She would be
positively amazed did you suggest religion to be
anything less than a gloomy affair : she is quite
horrified that the Salvation Army is conducted on
lines as though religion were a kind of perpetual
beanfeast. Religion can always be a gloomy affair for
rich people, but if it is to attract poor people it must
be cheerful. The poor, having no treasure on earth,
are quite likely to enjoy a cheerful spiritual hunt for

the treasure that is promised them in heaven. And
Shaw himself admits that he has been severely mauled
by the critics for allowing the Salvation Army to
conduct their religious exercises with a minimum of
gloomy piety. Lady Britomart expresses quite
forcibly the appalling and popular position that to
be religious it is quite necessary to be gloomy, and
not seldom cantankerous. The reason that many
religious people are cantankerous is that they often
do not believe what they say they believe. So Lady
Britomart is quite angry that Barbara suggests
religion is the reverse of unpleasing. Lady Britomart
feels that such a position is distinctly bad form. The
best families do not do it : they prefer to eat the
Body of God and drink His Blood and wail as they
do it. By all means let them wail if they wish, so
long as they do not wish other people to wail with
them.

LADY BRITOMART. Really, Barbara, you go on as if
religion were a pleasant subject. Do have some
sense of propriety.

An argument between Undershaft, the millionaire,
and Shirley, one of the Salvation Army "pick-ups,"
gives Shaw an excellent chance of a piece of typical
Shavian repartee. And there is a very beastly truth
in it, as there is in most of Shaw's smart dialogue.
Shirley is amazingly well drawn here : the disgruntled
workman hovering between life and death on meat
once a week, knows that his only chance of getting
even with the rich is to indulge in the kind of abuse
which says, " Well, I may not have your riches, but

thank God I haven't got your conscience." This is
shattering enough, the only unfortunate part of the
whole affair being that the rich man is usually not
only richer in money but richer in powers of dialectic.
So when Shirley hurls the usual question that people
like Shirley do hurl at rich men, " How did you get
your millions except by sweating the poor or cheating
the honest ? " Undershaft manages to twist the
argument, not perhaps giving it any moral significance
at all, but leaving Shirley tied up in a very effectual
knot. It is, of course, a poor game for the rich to
argue with the poor, for the rich win every time until
the Last Day when all argument will cease at the sound
of the universal notes of the great Réveillé. However, Undershaft finds the chance given him by Shirley
too good to be missed and his reply is sparkling
Shavianism.

> SHIRLEY. Who made your millions for you ? Me
> and my like. What's kep' us poor ? Keeping
> you rich. I wouldn't have your conscience, not
> for all your income.
> UNDERSHAFT. I wouldn't have your income, not
> for all your conscience, Mr. Shirley.

Turning back again to the teaching of the Salvation
Army, Shaw gives us a very excellent example of its
intensely practical theology. Barbara is really a
splendid Salvationist : she can give tangibility to
every kind of spiritual emotion ; she can apologise for
the existence of the soul by means of a rather trite
sentence quite as effectively as the admirable gentleman who on eight Sunday afternoons in St. Mary's,

Oxford, delivers the Bampton lectures. Bill Walker, possibly a little exaggerated as a character, nevertheless is true enough to type when he is perfectly certain that he has no soul because he hasn't seen it. Most of us would probably be much more certain that we had no soul if we did see it ! Cusins, a type of character that we do not find very often in Shaw's plays, a very typical student with all the gentleness and bad temper of the student combined, remarks that a consideration of what a Greek would do in certain circumstances will provide quite an excellent exercise for Walker's soul. Walker, spending his life in surroundings about as soulless as any could be, the further back streets in the back areas in London, naturally enough denies the remotest possibility of his possessing a soul. Barbara, as I have said already, retorts with that kind of invincible logic which is not an argument in itself but substantiates the non-possibility of the other's alleged argument.

> BILL. Rot ! There ain't no sach a thing as a soul. Ah kin you tell wether I've a soul or not ? You never seen it.
> BARBARA. I've seen it hurting you when you went against it.

. . . . . .

Towards the end of *Major Barbara* Shaw dashes up to the climax of the whole argument of the play—the argument that poverty is a crime, the lesser argument that religious bodies must depend for their financial support upon money derived from questionable

sources.   Undershaft not only continually defends his
action of becoming a millionaire by the creation of
deadly weapons of war, but turns round and brings
home the argument of the criminality of poverty very
forcibly to Barbara.   If it hadn't been for his enterprise and money, where would she have been ?   If it
hadn't been for his money, wouldn't she have been
one of the Salvation Army rescued instead of a leader
in that very excellent body ?   Undershaft, with something like a sudden kind of vicious triumph, the
triumph of a man when he sees his argument for vice
turning into an argument for virtue, brings the
matter slap home to Barbara.   " My dear young
lady," he seems to say, " with all your contempt for
my munition factory, with all your contempt for my
brain which can produce weapons which will make
war possible from my own drawing-room, with all
your contempt for my model city of workers, with all
your contempt for my having chosen riches rather
than poverty—I have not only saved your soul, but
I have saved it from the seven deadly sins.   You may
well look bewildered, for my seven deadly sins are
not the seven deadly sins labelled by the churches but
the seven deadly sins which can only find salvation
through money."

UNDERSHAFT. Yes, the deadly seven. Food, cloth-
ing, firing, rent, taxes, respectability, and
children. Nothing can lift those seven millstones from Man's neck but money ; and the
spirit cannot soar until the millstones are lifted.
I lifted them from your spirit. I enabled

Barbara to become Major Barbara ; and I saved her from the crime of poverty.

Immediately after Undershaft has delivered himself of this speech, Cusins asks the question to which Shaw finds it so necessary to reply. The position that is surprising to Cusins is that poverty is not a misfortune but a definite crime. Undershaft's reply is so important and so much the essence of Shavianism on the poverty problem, that I quote it in its entirety.

UNDERSHAFT. The worst of crimes. All the other crimes are virtues beside it : all the other dishonours are chivalry itself by comparison. Poverty blights whole cities ; spreads horrible pestilences ; strikes dead the very souls of all who come within sight, sound, or smell of it. What you call crime is nothing ; a murder here and a theft there, a blow now and a curse then : what do they matter ? they are only the accidents and illnesses of life ; there are not fifty genuine professional criminals in London. But there are millions of poor people, abject people, dirty people, ill-fed, ill-clothed people. They poison us morally and physically ; they kill the happiness of society ; they force us to do away with our own liberties and to organise unnatural cruelties for fear they should rise against us and drag us down into their abyss. Only fools fear crime ; we all fear poverty. Pah ! you talk of your half-saved ruffian in West Ham ; you accuse me of dragging his soul back to perdition. Well, bring him to me here ; and I will drag his soul back again to salvation for you.   Not by words and dreams, but by thirty-eight shillings a week, a sound house in a handsome street, and a permanent job.   In three weeks he will have a fancy waistcoat ; in three months a tall hat and a chapel sitting ; before the end of the year he will shake hands with a duchess at a Primrose League meeting, and join the Conservative Party.

The argument is certainly true up to a point.   But it is the acceptance of a second best.   Get rid of poverty by all means, treat it as the crime against the Holy Ghost, but do not be content with an alternative which simply (in this Undershaft example) substitutes for poverty non-poverty through the successful making of vile weapons of war.   The Shavian argument is all right as it stands, and we can all sympathise with his position that the worst crime is poverty, but let us get rid of both poverty and war munitions, not the elimination of the one criminal state of society by the imposition of an even more reprehensible state of affairs.

Major Barbara, partly an indictment of the Salvation Army, partly a defence of it, should make most people incline to an admiration of the Salvation Army rather than to a hostility towards it.

N

CHAPTER II

SHAW AND CHILDREN

NOTHING could be more natural than for a reformer to be interested in children. With the birth of a child there is let loose upon the world the possibility of an energy that may depart from the energy displayed by its forebears. The old doggerel, a kind of subtle political quip, which intimated that every child born alive was either a little Liberal or a little Conservative, might be expanded to include the possibility that it might also be an evolutionist. We have but the slenderest chance of reforming adult people ; their ways are too stolid, their income too fixed by their opinions, their opinions largely persuaded by their incomes. In the case of children there is more chance. They have not yet become set in their opinions although our rascally system of education tends to bring up not a number of individuals but a number of automata who will merely be the means of carrying on fixed rules however much they may suffer thereby. Quite generally our treatment of children is shocking. The English child is the worst educated in the world. The Shavian indictment that education teaches nothing worth knowing has more truth than might be expected in such a sweeping generalisation. We do treat children very badly. We are irritated with them if they are

184

children : we are more irritated with them if they are precocious. We force them into a certain channel of thought however unsuitable such a channel of thought may be for their particular temperament. Our public schools are often unduly the manufactory of snobs : our private schools fill the pockets of schoolmasters.

We give an intellectual training when the whole of life merely demonstrates that intellectual prowess is viewed with suspicion by the mass of men who care for nothing but money-grubbing. Should a child show any sincere signs of wishing to become an artist the family is inclined to believe that there must be a bad strain somewhere. Should a child be really clever he is so crammed to make an advertisement for his school that more often than not he ends in the gutter. Should a child be really dull he leaves school hated by his schoolmasters and despised by his parents. The result is then that he either becomes a Prime Minister living in Downing Street or a popular novelist living in Baker Street. There does seem, then, to be some kind of dilemma, that neither the clever nor the dull boy can expect to get very much out of professional education.

Now Bernard Shaw, apart from his particular preface dealing with children, parents, and education, dealt, of course, with the subject in *Mrs. Warren's Profession*. I am not concerned with the profession of Mrs. Warren, nor am I concerned with Miss Warren's intellectual love affair. What I am concerned with is Miss Warren complaining, as she does by her attitude all through the play, that university educa-

tion is no effective armour to withstand the blows
delivered by life.   It is never meant to.   University
education stands for the something that may be
called refusal to be beaten.   When Miss Warren,
firmly enthusiastic concerning syllogisms and basic
principles, suddenly hears that her vulgar mother is
nothing less than a dirty little keeper of brothels, she
is not so much dismayed by the news as by the fact
that her intellectual training gives her no ready
response to such a situation.   She is much more
inclined to howl abuse at her education than to howl
abuse at her mother.   Shaw interprets Miss Warren's
attitude to be a proof of the inadequacy of the
academic preparation for life.   It is, I am afraid, true
that the universities provide excellent education if the
world were a university !   The university standard is
one of fair play and sportsmanship.   The standard of
the world is praise God, cheat your neighbour, and
get to the front yourself.   The university education
loves learning for its own sake : the world loves
learning for its economic possibilities.   The university
studies God to try to know Him : the world studies
im to turn Him into a kind of contemptible fool to
be propitiated by protestations of allegiance.

Shaw makes no bones about it that our treatment
of children is criminally wrong, that most, if not all,
parents are either fools or blackguards, while nothing
can exceed Shaw's detestation of the school system.
There is, of course, a tremendous amount that is
wrong, but it is quite easy to fail to see the other side.
Shaw's chief annoyance with parents is that they
bring up children according to a fixed rule.   He is

angry that parents feel it incumbent upon themselves to bring up a child in the way it should go. And at present Shaw inclines to the opinion that all ways, so far, have proved to be the wrong way. Again, the reason, as he says, is not necessarily negligence or indifference on the part of parents, but a hard stolid fact that nobody knows which way a child ought to go. Let it have its own way and, more often than not, it becomes a mere shiftless dependent. Force it to go our way and more often than not it becomes an anarchical independent. We take scrupulous care of our children, and they become rotters : we take little care of them and they become saints. There seems to be no definite road.

At this particular time when there is a tremendous controversy concerning the size of families, it is interesting to discover Shaw's position about this. He is in favour of large families. Why ? Not to give the state more taxpayers ; not to propitiate the lust of the churches who demand more believers ; not to have more manhood so that the next war can be fought on a bigger scale ; but because members of a large family have a better chance of being brought up well since they have a better chance of bringing themselves up without undue parental interference. Shaw has the greatest horror of the child being brought up entirely by his parents. If we are to understand fairly this hostility to parental rule, which is so apparent in Shaw's writings, we must understand his fundamental position with regard to the child. Every child is to Shaw someone on whom the Life Force wishes to experiment. The child should, then,

be allowed to do what it likes because it is not a free
agent—it is simply in reality a slave of the Life Force.
When the parent with all the goodwill in the world
tries to bring up a child in the way he feels it ought
to go, he is, probably quite unconsciously, unless he
has steeped himself in the Shavian philosophy,
helping to defeat the plans of the Life Force.   So
Shaw puts his fundamental position :

> " If you once allow yourself to regard a child
> as so much material for you to manufacture into
> any shape that happens to suit your fancy you
> are defeating the experiment of the Life Force.
> You are assuming that the child does not know
> its own business and that you do.   In this you
> are sure to be wrong : the child feels the drive of
> the Life Force (often called the will of God) ; and
> you cannot feel it for him."

Shaw soon hits upon a fundamental attitude that
many of us, without in the least disliking children,
adopt towards them.   We find them a nuisance ; they
have a habit of blackleading the drawing-room carpet ;
they have a curious habit of delighting in dustbin
lids ;   they are eager to drink ink ;   they are wise
enough to think that manuscripts should be torn up
and not published.   Shaw discovers that there is a
very great difficulty about the care of children.
People of high character and intelligence more often
than not will not be bothered with children at all :
persons of meagre intelligence will let a child do
almost anything it likes so long as they are not
worried.   The highly intelligent father cannot stand

a child in the room because it wants to know why a cow is a cow. The nursemaid is annoyed by the same question, not because she doesn't know the answer (she has not sufficient intelligence to know that), but because she wants to read a book or carry out some domestic duty. The fundamental position, then, assumed by Shaw is that our first reaction to a child is to find it a nuisance; our second reaction is to hand it over to a rather gross, underpaid nursemaid who simply has no interest in the child except in so far as it means that she keeps her place in service. Consequently, at a very early age the child grows up with the accumulating feeling that nobody quite wants it. It is not wanted in the drawing-room and it has no wish to be there except for the fact that ornaments make a nice smash when they are broken; it knows that in the nursery as long as it does not worry the nursemaid it may play soldiers or pick its nose so long as it keeps out of the way. Again, one of the great difficulties of treating children is that some of them are younger than we are. Quite a number in this twentieth century are older than their parents. We cannot get into the mind of a child any more than the child can get into the mind of an old man. A child cannot understand smoking a pipe and reading the *Times* any more than an old man can understand why it is his young grandson will carry the cat all round the house upside down. Shaw by means of one or two quite simple examples deals admirably with this difference in age problem.

    " Old people and young people cannot walk at

the same pace without distress and final loss of health to one of the parties. When they are sitting indoors they cannot endure the same degrees of temperature and the same supplies of fresh air. Even if the main factors of noise, restlessness, and inquisitiveness are left out of count, children can stand with indifference sights, sounds, smells, and disorders that would make an adult of fifty utterly miserable ; whilst, on the other hand, such adults find a tranquil happiness in conditions which to children mean unspeakable boredom."

And, of course, the whole folly of our civilisation is that all people of all ages are stuffed into one house and in the case of the masses of the poor are stuffed into one room. Thus you have in one corner of the room the father dying of cancer ; in another the elder daughter looking after her illegitimate baby ; while in a third the unfortunate mother endeavours to prevent herself from becoming a mere playground for vermin. In such an atmosphere in our appalling big cities do we bring up children who ought to know nothing of the horrors of life until they are able to cope with them. No matter, be the home a hovel or a castle, Shaw sees children never getting a fair chance. In the homes of the poor they receive either neglect or abuse from their parents : in the homes of the rich they scarcely know their parents ; and in after life, quite naturally, they give all their affections to the old lady living in a pensioner's cottage who used to tuck them up in bed and dispel the goblins with a beneficent nightlight. This in itself is an excellent thing as long as it does not carry with it a somewhat indefinite dislike of parents.

There is, then, the other side which Shaw deals with in his preface to *Misalliance*, that is, when children are the recipients of an exaggerated affection. This exaggerated affection seems to Shaw to lead to a false kind of family affection, the kind of family affection which feels that brothers must protect brothers, not because in the real sense there is any brotherly affection but simply because they are brothers. Very amusingly does Shaw write of the type of mother who kisses her child a dozen times because she is so thankful that after the twelfth kiss she will be able to pack the child off to the nursery while she prepares for an evening of delirious boredom with her " something in the city " husband. It all leads, as Shaw remarks, to the same thing, that while adults and children live together one of the two will be miserable. In this way, then, does Shaw put the position—a picture which proves, although no proof is needed, that most mothers are tremendous humbugs:

> " The true cry of the kind mother, after her little rosary of kisses is ' Run away, darling.' It is nicer than ' Hold your noise, you young devil ; or it will be the worse for you ' ; but fundamentally it means the same thing : that if you compel an adult and a child to live in one another's company either the adult or the child will be miserable. There is nothing whatever unnatural or wrong or shocking in this fact ; and there is

no harm in it if only it be sensibly faced and
provided for.   The mischief that it does at present
is produced by our efforts to ignore it under a
heap of sentimental lies and false pretences."

We had much better realise that there is a time
when children are a nuisance to adults and a still
smaller time when adults are not a nuisance to
children.   How irritating it is when father bear is just
about to bring home a sackful of chocolate cream from
the fairy wood that the story has to stop because it is
bed-time and dinner will soon be on the table, while
the child isn't quite sure after all whether that shadow
at the nursery window isn't really the beastly bear.
In such circumstances the sack of chocolate cream is
not quite a compensation.

Quite the most important part of Shaw's preface
on parents and children is that which has to do with
the problem of school.   Shaw dislikes many things ;
he hates school ; he dislikes the prison system ; he
loathes the school system ; he dislikes slavery,
whether of the intellect or of the soul ; he abominates
the slavery of school ; he dislikes the coarse vul-
garities of prison life ; he detests the mental torture
of schools.

It is difficult if not impossible to find anything in
the school system that Shaw can consider of good
account.   There is a certain amount of truth in his
comparison between a prison and a school.   Both
curtail liberty : both present the spectacle of authority
battling against defiance ; boys and prisoners are
inarticulate rebels.   The schoolboy hates the school-

master : the prisoner generally hates the governor ; neither dares show open resentment. The result is not quite the same. Coming out of school, the schoolboy leaves his grudge behind him : coming out of prison the prisoner hates society to the end of his days. The more society tries to help the prisoner, the more he hates it, for the prisoner who returns to the world has nothing left to him but his grudge, and if society attempts to lessen that it will earn (perfectly unfairly) contempt and dislike. It is an insult to treat a returned prisoner with violence ; it is a worse insult to treat him with condescending courtesy. He should be treated as he was treated before he went to prison—should have just the treatment that we mete out to all our citizens, a mere indifferent contempt over which the citizen can rise or under which he may fall.

A certain amount of autobiographical matter shows us that Shaw in writing of school is writing of something that he has experienced. He commits something that would be to a large number of men a breach of good manners. You may steal ; you may kill ; you may commit rape ; you may look at your neighbour's wife with adulterous eyes, but there are two things you must not do. You must not speak against your school and you must not shoot foxes. But that is not the same thing as criticising the school in which you passed your dreadful and unbelievable boyhood. Shaw's chief complaint is that the masters he was under did not care whether he learnt anything or not. This is, I think, a common enough criticism. Masters, when all is said and done, are merely wage

earners. Like the boys under them, their principal
wish is for the clock to strike twelve. They are not
interested in the dull boys : they are not a potential
advertisement for the school ; dull boys are usually
sullen and morose ; they are always dishonest and
they nearly always have objectionable parents.
Shaw goes still further and says that his schooling
did him a great deal of harm. There again probably
many men who, without in the least wishing to
disparage their school, would say the same thing.
The life of many boys at school is a dualism of fear—
the fear of ridicule, if not actual violence, from the
masters : the fear of almost certain violence from the
other boys. Many boys simply discover at school
long before they ought to that the mass of humanity
is hostile towards them and they carry this impression,
true or false, into the outside world where humanity
is not hostile but merely indifferent. There are
probably more people than might be imagined who
would prefer the hostility of the school to the cool and
calculating coldness of ordinary humanity.

Having, then, assured us that he hated school, that
he was definitely neglected at school, that he learnt
nothing, Shaw tells us what he actually did attain to
in the matter of any kind of learning. It is impossible
here to go into the vexed question of the economic
utility of learning Latin and Greek. As a personal
opinion I believe the learning of these two languages
to be most necessary. It is almost impossible to
understand classical history without Latin ; it is quite
impossible to understand the Christian story without
knowing Greek. Latin and Greek are also a very

excellent armour against the atrocious doctrines taught in commercial schools, where successful business men deal with decent men and women, turning them into crawling little money-grubbers. It is a pity, although not surprising, that Shaw has such a contempt for the learning of Latin and Greek. It of course accounts for his uncritical attitude to certain questions. With a burst of anger he tells us what he was taught at school. It is, I am afraid true, but it is as well to remember that many lessons have no need to be remembered. Instead of learning French, German, and Italian, as Shaw would have wished, he writes : " I was taught lying, dishonourable submission to tyranny, dirty stories, a blasphemous habit of treating love and maternity as obscene jokes, hopelessness, evasion, derision, cowardice, and all the blackguard shifts by which the coward intimidates other cowards." Certainly Shaw has not remembered any of his lessons !

We may, then, look at some of the points that Shaw feels ought to be taught in any school system.

. . . . .

Generally speaking Shaw in looking at a school curriculum convinces himself that the school programme represents, not an effort to make useful citizens, but is a programme devised to keep children out of mischief. If it fails on the first point, it certainly fails on the second also. At boarding schools, at any rate, children not only get into mischief, but they get into most deadly infamy. The conversation of an ordinary school dormitory is quite unprintable, when, as a matter of fact, it would be an excellent thing if the ordinary conversation of a school dormitory were broadcast by the B.B.C. Shaw, then, is irritated that schools, as a whole, do not teach economics or political science. The chief reason for this is that there are very few masters capable of teaching these subjects. A lesser reason is that, while schools inculcate the necessity of playing for the side, they seldom, if ever, inculcate the necessity of living for the state. Any kind of socialism must be banned as leading to the overthrow of the state, when, as a matter of fact, the most common cause through history of the overthrow of the state has been the constitutional monarchs. Yet another reason is that too economically minded schoolboys would upset the crass conservatism of their fathers. They live for themselves and their children : why should not their children do the same thing ? " Caesar leaving his winter quarters was good enough for me at school : why should John be worried with questions of rent, divorce, and landlordism ? " Shaw goes so far as to suggest that the lack of econ- omic teaching in the schools is, in reality, done purposely. There is, so Shaw sees, a scholastic opposition to teaching children the law of equivalent consumption and production. Thus he writes con- cerning the fundamental economic truth that should be taught in all schools :

> " The most important, simple, fundamental economic truth to impress on a child in com- plicated civilisations like ours is the truth that whoever consumes goods or services without

producing by personal effort the equivalent of what he or she consumes, inflicts on the community precisely the same injury that a thief produces, and would, in any honest state, be treated as a thief however full his or her pockets might be of money made by other people."

This, then, is for Shaw one of the great weaknesses of the school system—the suppression of the teaching of economics. The other great weakness in our schools is for Shaw the suppression of the subject of sex. The reason is not the same as for the economic teaching suppression, that suppression being in the interest of capitalism, the other suppression being a much more sincere one—a certain desire to avoid a complicated and troublesome subject, the teaching of which is always a matter of violent controversy. Shaw believes that sex teaching should be given in the schools by qualified people if only for the simple reason that it is better that it should be taught scientifically than learnt from other children by subterranean methods. This may not be a very vital reason, but it is at least a reasonable one.

We have, then, so far examined a few of Shaw's criticisms of the relationships between children and parents and children and school. The remainder of this chapter can well be devoted to a consideration of something of the constructive proposals that Bernard Shaw suggests with regard to the problems we have been discussing. Shaw admits straight away that he has no system that will replace all the other systems. There is no reason why he should have one. In no branch of learning have we yet arrived at the position when one system will suit everybody. Bernard Shaw approaches his constructive policy by asking what are the rights of children. The child has first of all the simple right to live, which really means that within reason it has the same rights of liberty as the adult person. At the same time the child's right to live implies a certain responsibility to society. It must live without wasting other people's time. In a word, it must be brought up to be a reasonable and useful member of society. If it is a little precocious it is all Bernard Shaw's fault !

Shaw proceeds from his rather commonplace generalisation—a child's right to live—to asking whether a child should be expected to earn its own living. He dismisses, of course, as absurd any question of child labour as it was understood a hundred years or more ago. What he aims at is that the child shall do some kind of work for its own sake and for that of the community, work in school being, in his opinion, merely a waste of time. The child, then, is to become at once some kind of a working member of society, grown up long before its age, a kind of super child, in reality nothing more than a super prig. So I do not think that most people will consider Shaw's suggestion that children should work at an early age of very much advantage. However, this is the Shavian position and Shaw writes thus :

" There is every reason why a child should not be allowed to work for commercial profit or for the support of its parents at the expense of its own future ; but there is no reason whatever why a child should not do some work for its own sake and that of the community if it can be shown that both it and the community will be the better for it."

The strong probability is that neither the child nor the community will be the better for it. Shaw continues at some length to evolve his plan of work for children. But it is not really of sufficient importance to merit further consideration. The school system is pretty bad in many ways but not so bad as the system would be without any school. It is always the habit of the person who considers himself a practical reformer as does Bernard Shaw to sneer at anything that tends towards scholastic polish. By all means let us have practical schools, but not schools that do not make their scholars practise Latin and Greek.

There is, of course, a good deal of truth in the Shavian cynicism that the real and essential reason that our parents send us to public schools is that we may learn manners. The public schools do give a man a certain polished manner which is usually a mixture of courtesy and offensiveness. The public school manner is not easy of definition. It is just that slight expression of superiority which makes the public school man so unpopular in the workaday world. He gains this manner from the fact that he is always taught to look upon his school as *the* school and to look down politely on anyone else. In other words the public school manner is a manner of tradition, an unconscious handing on. Thus Shaw

o

hits the right nail on the head when he demands that
the main function of the public schools is to teach the
manners that are customary in a certain class of
society. The public school manner, offensive as it
frequently is, is not so offensive as the customary lack
of manners of the modern person. So Shaw writes of
the people who, knowing the public schools and
universities to be pretty rotten places, still support
them by the sending of their children. Shaw's reason
is in most cases correct enough !

> "And peers who tell you that our public
> schools are rotten through and through, and that
> our Universities ought to be razed to the founda-
> tions, send their sons to Eton and Oxford,
> Harrow and Cambridge, not only because there
> is nothing else to be done, but because these
> places, though they turn out blackguards and
> ignoramuses and boobies galore, turn them out
> w th the habits and manners of the society they
> belong to. Bad as those manners are in many
> respects, they are better than no manners at all.
> And no individual or family can possibly teach
> them. They can be acquired only by living in
> an organised community in which they are
> traditional."

This chapter would be quite incomplete without a
reference to Shaw's position with regard to religious
teaching for children. His great point is that children
should be taught some kind of religious toleration.
Shaw believes that children should be taught that
if there are Christians there are also Mohammedans,

Buddhists, Shintoists and other religious persons, who are just as honourable or dishonourable as the child's Christian father. Shaw goes on to say, as if he were making a new discovery, that children should be taught that those who believe in Allah have just as good a chance of salvation as those who believe in Christ. So he writes, but he has not really anything new to say in this respect, for no responsible teacher would assume for a moment that the followers of Allah were inferior to the followers of Christ. What they would teach would be that it seemed probable on historical evidence that Christ was more likely to be God than Allah. Certainly a child should be taught comparative religion, provided it has time to go into such an intricate subject.

> " It should be taught that Allah is simply the
> name by which God is known to Turks and
> Arabs who are just as eligible for salvation as any
> Christian."

This is, of course, reasonable enough, and should be objected to by no one.

.   .   .   .   .

Let us sum up a few of the points that Shaw deals with in his preface on Parents and Children. The system that receives his greatest hatred is the school system. It is, for him, merely a prison, in which no one is taught anything worth learning. At present Shaw sees that children are a nuisance to parents and parents are a nuisance to children. There must be, then, he asserts, some method by which children can enjoy the society of parents and parents can enjoy the society of children. Any kind of school should teach a child some kind of political economy ; it should teach him something about the question of sex, otherwise he will learn it from illegal sources. Religious teaching must insist on the necessity of religious toleration. Finally, whatever may be the details of any system created to teach children, liberty must be the foundation of it.

> " Liberty is the breath of life to nations ; and liberty is the one thing that parents, schoolmasters and rulers spend their lives in extirpating for the sake of an immediately quiet and finally disastrous life."

That is to say that parents, schoolmasters and rulers are essentially selfish, that children must be suppressed both in the home and in the school for the sake of the freedom from worry that adults desire. In many cases this is probably true : in many more cases it is probably false. Though Shaw does discover many weaknesses in the home and in the school which tend to cramp children, he seems too little inclined to emphasise the large number of people who do in all sincerity attribute all their success in after life to the care of their parents and their experiences during the period of education, whether at home or in school.

CHAPTER III

SAINT JOAN

IN some ways *Saint Joan* is the most un-Shavian of all Shaw's plays. Truly enough the play is problematical; it abounds in problematical situations; the voices that Joan of Arc heard; her distinct masculinity; the perplexing situations at her trial; her influence on history both French and English. But Shaw as it were gets a subject from outside himself. He is for the moment not only a playwright but a critic of history. He is writing historical drama, the drama that makes the theatre the attractive theatre of learning. All the way through *Saint Joan* Shaw is sympathetic to Joan of Arc. He sees her almost as a feminine counterpart of himself, smashing up her dull contemporaries by showing them the way they ought to go, dashing into the fray with a light-hearted contempt of danger—a figure symbolic of the type of person who is always outside the age.

When *Saint Joan* was produced in London some years ago many of the critics hailed it as the most outstanding play of the century and the most outstanding of Shaw's plays. The critics were both right and wrong. They were right in declaring *Saint Joan* to be a play lending distinction to the theatre: they were wrong in attributing to it a reward which said it was Shaw's best play. It was not Shaw's best play ; I am not sure that it was his second best play ; I am sure it was an extraordinarily good play. In my opinion it was distinctly inferior to *Man and Superman*, and I do not think it was superior to *Candida*. The essence of the whole thing was that it brought Shaw out in a new light. It proved that he knew a great deal more about the Church than he had ever shown us before. Shaw is almost pedantically careful to be fair. If we are to go back with him for an excursion into the Middle Ages, let our excursion be a critical one but a fair one. Shaw is determined to get into the mind of the peasant girl from Domrémy and also into the mind that lies behind the Catholic Church.

Probably the best method of dealing with Shaw's work on Saint Joan will be to consider first of all his critical preface concerning her and then to discuss the play, which is a logical sequel to his preface. Joan of Arc, born over five hundred years ago and canonised less than a dozen years ago, represents in a world of thought an almost quick process of evolution. Five hundred years is a small period in which a body like the Catholic Church will proceed from the condemnation of a girl for being a witch to the canonisation of her for being a saint. Thought moves slowly : ecclesiastical thought seldom catches it up. To represent such a change in thought it is very necessary to get back as deeply as possible into the minds of those who condemned Saint Joan, for, although it is not easily recognisable, the same mental attitude that condemned Joan of Arc as a witch canonised her five hundred years afterwards—the same mind working in

a different way, that nothing matters except the
well-being of the soul and the sovereignty of the
Church. But we shall come to this mental attitude
of the Church to Saint Joan later on.

. . . . .

The preface that Shaw writes about Saint Joan is
an extremely balanced survey of the eccentric French
girl and her uncongenial surroundings. Had Joan of
Arc lived to-day she would have been dreadfully disappointed at the entire lack of interest that she would
experience. Joan, like most great historical figures,
lived in an age which was both the right and the
wrong age for her. The wrongness of it sent her to
be burnt : the rightness of it allowed her to become
historical. Very wisely Bernard Shaw deals with the
question of Joan's good looks at the outset of his
preface. Her good looks or otherwise have no little
to do with getting a right estimate of her. Had she
been supremely beautiful she might easily have
forced her way to the front without the help of
external influences. Had she been hideous we might
believe much more strongly than we do in the mystical
agencies which were certainly the cause of her mag-
netism. I do feel all the way through that Shaw,
while wishing us to believe that there was a " something " about Joan in herself which marked her out,
implies that at the same time without some supernatural help she would not have caused all the
excitement she did. Apparently Joan was neither
pretty nor ugly : she was merely a woman. Shaw
tells us that her face could best be described as being
remarkable,

The social position of Joan is not particularly interesting nor perhaps particularly important. She came from the lower middle class which lives on farms in the country and in villas in the towns. It is probable that the county would have spoken to her in the street and been quite careful never to have her at the dinner table.

It is as well to go at once into the general reason why (a thing she could never understand) Joan always managed to be hated by the people she helped. Shaw puts the position concisely. They hated her because her very help showed up their weaknesses. When she found people who she was convinced were foolish, she made no bones about calling them so. Thus we at once get to an essential characteristic of Saint Joan. It is that she is never by any chance a diplomat. She never says what she does not mean. She never saw that sometimes it is as well not to let men who are wrong know that they are wrong. Had she been more diplomatic she would have lived longer and probably never lived in history at all. Thus Shaw points out the immaturity that always charac- terised Joan and made her her own worst enemy in circumstances where dialectic and tact were needed :

> " If she had been old enough to know the effect she was producing on the men whom she humiliated by being right when they were wrong, and had learned to flatter and manage them, she might have lived as long as Queen Elizabeth."

Joan's contemporaries disliked her because she was quite often right. The man who saves his country always receives from those he has saved hatred and contempt. Joan, like all big people, is hated by little people, and she is the more hated because she is a little person herself.

There is an interesting comparison which Shaw draws between Joan and Napoleon. Joan can never understand why she is unpopular : Napoleon can never give any reason why he should not be unpopular. When I die, he seems to say, all Europe will resound with the deep breathing of relief. What Saint Joan could never see was that the people she rescued were frightened of their rescuer. She rescues us to-day, they seem to say, to-morrow with her accursed voices she will drive us into the sea. Joan, as Shaw points out, belongs to those who die hated not so much by their enemies as by their friends. Few of us gain such an admirable distinction. Few of us are too uncommonplace to be hated by our friends. It may indeed be an epitaph to greatness that he died knowing that his friends dressed in deep black, rejoiced with a horrid joy.

At the end there are none to help Joan, for she has exposed the follies of her countrymen and they are furious that she has driven their enemies into the sea. Let her crown Charles in Rheims Cathedral and he will show his gratitude and curse her, that she, a mere peasant girl, a mere farm slut, a trafficker in voices, has dared to crown the King of France. She has saved her friends and she must be crucified : she has come to save France and she shall surely die for her presumption as the despised and rejected Carpenter was crucified for daring to save the world. So Shaw sees the inevitability of the hatred directed to Joan, the hatred that the dullard feels for the saviour who saves him because he cannot save himself.

> " Joan was burnt without a hand lifted on her own side to save her. The comrades she had led to victory and the enemies she had disgraced and defeated, the French King she had crowned and the English King whose crown she had kicked into the Loire, were equally glad to be rid of her."

Whether Joan was innocent or guilty is not for Shaw the supreme point at issue. The two points briefly are, firstly, that she received a remarkably fair trial from the Church and the Inquisition, and secondly, that posterity, witnessing the culmination of the whitewashing of Joan producing her canonisation, is inclined to put her judges unfairly on trial. Shaw has not the smallest sympathy with the type of mind which sees the judges in the Joan trial merely villains in a melodrama. The Bishop of Beauvais, the Inquisitor, tried Joan fairly. Her condemnation was a mere application of the inevitable logic of the Catholic Church. Her judges were much less prejudiced against their prisoner than many a modern judge.

The great difficulty, and it is a very ordinary difficulty, is to get a really accurate picture of Saint Joan, the canonisation of her inclining to a policy of whitewashing that is liable to obscure her character. The difficulty, then, for the modern historian is not

to wash the mud off Joan but to see through the
whitewash which is tending to veil her real personality. It is interesting to discover what qualities
Shaw suggests should be possessed by the future
historian of Saint Joan. He writes :

> " Her ideal biographer must be free from nine-
> teenth-century prejudices and biases ; must
> understand the Middle Ages, the Roman Catholic
> Church and the Holy Roman Empire much
> more intimately than our weak historians have
> ever understood them ; and must be capable of
> throwing off sex partialities and their romance,
> and regarding woman as the female of the human
> species, and not as a different kind of animal with
> specific charms and specific imbecilities."

Bernard Shaw seems to possess quite a number of
the attributes of his ideal biographer.

We must now turn to the extremely interesting and
important question of the voices that Joan heard and
the vision that she demanded that she saw. They
have been used to prove that she was mad, they have
been used to prove that she was a saint, they have
seldom been used to prove that the supernatural, if
it exists at all, is dull enough to be really utilitarian.
The essential point to remember in any consideration
of the voices that came to Saint Joan is that she was
a woman endowed with a vast power of imagination.
Had she not been a saint she would probably have
been a popular novelist, she might even have written
a play on the logic of the Inquisition. Bernard Shaw
sees that Saint Joan was one of those people possessing
such a vivid imagination that an idea became really

tangible. Plato's theory of ideas gave a distinct tangibility to the ideas making them something that, in popular language, could be determined as concrete. Joan lived in a world in which her ideas (brought to her by the voices and visions) were so tangible that they could be actually experienced and actually assumed bodily condition. Even the least imaginative of us can so dwell with an idea that it certainly seems to assume shape and occupy space. The man who commits murder and remarks to the magistrate who is already in his second childhood that he saw red, probably has seen some kind of concrete image to himself, at any rate, which is red. The first point, then, is that in the popular sense of the term (and the term is much more philosophical than many people imagine) Joan's visions and voices were real, even if they merely assumed that reality by reason of a vivid and vast imagination.

The second point that Shaw emphasises, and perfectly rightly, is that, in spite of her voices and visions, Joan was singularly sane. They were merely her way of personifying her imagination. Of course they may have been actual revelations from a supernatural source. There is, I think, no evidence whatever that they were either voices from an evil supernatural agency or that they were the hallucinations that would be part of the make-up of a mad woman. The real and essential point, whatever the origin of the voices, is that they gave Joan invariably reasonable advice and appeared to be possessed by an agency (even if the agency be merely Joan's imagination) rational and healthy.

Carrying the subject a little further, Shaw believes that Joan was what Francis Galton would call a visualiser.

There was a parallel between her and arithmeticians who are able to perform feats of memory not possible to non-visualisers. Let us leave it then that Joan saw imaginary saints with emphasis on the word "imaginary" and on the word "saw."

We come now to a characteristic of Joan that was much more strange to her contemporaries than it is to us. We are becoming, if we have not quite become, accustomed to the masculine woman. We are much more surprised to-day by the womanly woman! We are not in the least surprised by the woman who expresses a wish to lead an army corps into battle. Joan's contemporaries were. The question has now to be considered why it was that Joan elected to wear military dress and masculine dress. Shaw gives us the answer. Joan's masculine dress fitted in with the exigencies of the situation. It hid to some reasonable degree Joan's sex. A masculine and military dress made her passage through the country swarming with bands of hostile marauders safer than it would have been if she had adopted female attire of the conventional kind. So far, then, Shaw sees that up to a point Joan's masculine mode of dress was not an eccentric gesture nor even a gesture of "showing off," but merely a conformation to a vital necessity. But that is not all the problem. As Shaw emphasises in his preface, Joan wore masculine dress when she might conceivably have been content with the normal dress of her sex. Why, asks Shaw, does Joan on almost every occasion behave in a manner diverse from the conventional manners that society expects from a woman, and particularly the society of Joan's epoch ? The answer, says Shaw, is a perfectly simple one. Joan was the type of woman who must have sighed all her life and exclaimed with an exclamation unusually sincere, " If only I had been a man ! " Here, then, is Shaw's solution to the funny little puzzle, the puzzle of her trousers, the puzzle of her presents of swords and armour, the puzzle of her perfectly thoughtless habit of sleeping with her escort of soldiers. She was purely and simply one of those women who want to lead a man s life. This type of woman is " to be found wherever there are armies on foot or navies on the seas, serving in male disguise, eluding detection for astonishingly long periods, and sometimes, no doubt, escaping it entirely."

One more question has to be considered before we turn to the play itself. It has been alleged by historians of the type who will jump to the most obvious and quite often erroneous conclusions without troubling to go into any kind of historical comparison that Joan was possessed of certain rather vague suicidal tendencies. It is true, as Shaw points out, that Joan attempted to escape from captivity by jumping down some sixty feet from Beaurevoir Castle. But this impetuous act does not in the very smallest degree postulate an element of suicidism in Joan's character. Joan was the type of person who deliberately preferred the risk of death or death to captivity. She is but a quite commonplace type of

character to be found in military history. Wellington
treated cannon balls as a goalkeeper treats cannon-
ball shots. Nelson refused to cover up his medals
while directing operations from his quarter deck on
the *Victory*. A hundred thousand soldiers in a
hundred thousand wars have preferred the " no
surrender " stand to captivity in or behind the
enemies' lines. There is, then, no reason whatever to
believe that Joan possessed suicidal impulses.

What type of girl, then, is it that Shaw would wish
us to see? Something like this. A country girl
belonging to the lower middle class. A girl endowed
with great strength of mind and of parallel strength
of body. She was a person of a calculating nature.
She was ever diffident as to her responsibility for her
own success and ever attributed it to the voices and
visions that came to her. As an actual military
commander she had an obvious belief in artillery.
She believed that sieges were won by waiting ; one
side would have to give up in the end and the besiegers
would be less likely to because of their possibilities of
exit to the rear of the army. In no sense does Shaw
feel that Joan was romantic. She was no more
impressed by talking to the Dauphin than she was by
talking to one of the private soldiers. She felt all
men were equal and perhaps she thought most of
them were equally stupid. She refused to allow
disreputable language among her soldiers and she
would not tolerate the armies of loose women to
follow her troops—the armies of loose women who
were always to be found in evidence behind the Allied
armies in the Peninsula Wars. She had, apparently,

but one kind of religious oath, " En nom de." She
was ever a leader of people, the apostle waging war
against the Jeremiahs of her country. She was ever
the tearing, hurrying, saviour fighting for God and
La France.

> " She talked to and dealt with people of all
> classes, from labourers to kings, without embar-
> rassment or affectation and got them to do what
> she wanted when they were not afraid or corrupt.
> She could coax and she could hustle, her tongue
> having a soft side and a sharp edge. She was
> very capable : a born boss."

Such is the Shavian picture of the Maid of Orleans.
It is a picture characterised by Shaw's perpetual
refusal to ignore small points. His ambition to treat
Joan as an historical figure and not as either a heroine
of melodrama or a saint of a cathedral window does
no little to help him to give us such a rational picture
of the indomitable French girl who raised the Siege
of Orleans, crowned the Dauphin King of France,
defied the Inquisition, refused to accept captivity
rather than burning, and finally caused the Catholic
Church to reverse her condemnation of her as a
heretic and bestow upon her the everlasting light of
canonisation.

.   .   .   .   .

All through the play Bernard Shaw is most careful
to show that Joan always has about her some magnetic
attraction. She is important before she is important.
She has a magnetic influence long before she obtains

one by her remarkable achievements. She is a hussy, but she is a divine hussy. She has a habit of ever treating everybody as though she were their equal, a condescending gesture considering how superior she is to them really. Never for one moment through the play does Joan cease from insisting that she is directly sent by God. She treats the Deity with that kind of good-natured familiarity which characterises saints. God is on her side ; He will help her to lead her armies to victory ; He will help her crown the Dauphin in the great church of Rheims ; He will come to her when she is burning at the stake and will take her away. Joan moves with God in a delightful and easy kind of fellowship. She is His daughter, even if it be admitted that she is a little bit troublesome.

When Joan first introduces herself to Robert she at once emphasises the divinity of her mission. Robert, as is only natural, misunderstands her. How dare she, a mere common peasant girl, give him orders. Shaw is dealing with that kind of misunderstanding which it is always Joan's lot to put up with. Robert has but little imagination : he is the typical country squire ; he cannot see beyond the gates of the park, his petty kingdom over which he will assert despotic sway. And yet here is this wretched little slip of a village girl ordering him to provide her with a horse, armour, and some soldiers. And he is to provide them, for it is a direct order from her Lord. Insolence ! But the orders happen to be from the Lord who is King of Heaven. The deadly clash between Joan and Robert is clearly indicated in this preliminary meeting between them. Already there is

P

an indication of the type of girl Joan is, the girl who
will stand up to anything and anybody, because the
saints will stand with her.

> JOAN. Good morning, captain squire. Captain!
> you are to give me a horse and armour and some
> soldiers, and send me to the Dauphin. Those
> are your orders from my Lord.
> ROBERT. Orders from *your* lord! And who the
> devil may *your* lord be? Go back to him, and
> tell him that I am neither duke nor peer at his
> orders; I am squire of Baudricourt; and I take
> no orders except from the king.
> JOAN. Yes, squire; that is all right. My Lord is
> the King of Heaven.

I always feel that Shaw wishes to show that even
Joan herself is not quite certain what her voices
really are. When she is asked about them she main-
tains that obstinate attitude which is characteristic of
the person who thoroughly believes in the reality of
an experience even if it be not entirely empirical, but
is never quite sure of being able to pass that belief on
satisfactorily. Joan is always aware that she is up
against not exactly scoffers but those who would
reduce every experience to the realms of materialism.
She can fight very excellently the English soldiers;
she can fight much less excellently the sceptical
doubts of her opponents. She is quite convinced
that her messages do come from God, but she does
not in any way rule out the use of the imagination,
for, in her opinion, God speaks tangibly to the
imaginative faculty. Even if her voices are really

subjective, they are also objective. That is where
she departs from her sceptical unbelievers. They will
admit that the voices and visions and messages are
subjective, but they cannot see or they will not see
that they may be objective as well, even if the process
is, as it seems to me the process is to Joan, the objective creating the stimulus while the subjective,
harmonising with the aspirations of the objective,
fertilises the messages in her brain. ' This, I think, is
brought out by Shaw in the lines I quote here, when
Robert, with all that superficiality which characterises
the materialistic thinker, is quite certain that he has
destroyed the reality of Joan's visions and voices by
saying with a loud shout of intolerant tyranny, " But,
my dear little peasant girl, these voices that you hear
and these visions that you see are merely your
imagination—were I to speak to you philosophically,
I would say that they were subjective and not
objective." To which, as I say, Joan replies in effect
that her visions and voices are, philosophically treated,
both subjective and objective, or rather a combination
of the harmonious blending of the two energies.

ROBERT. What did you mean when you said that
St. Catherine and St. Margaret talked to you
every day ?
JOAN. They do.
ROBERT. What are they like ?
JOAN. I will tell you nothing about that ; they
have not given me leave.
ROBERT. But you actua'ly see them ; and they
talk to you just as I am talking to you ?

JOAN. No! it is quite different. I cannot tell you ;
you must not talk to me about my voices.

ROBERT. How do you mean ? voices ?

JOAN. I hear voices telling me what to do. They
come from God.

ROBERT. They come from your imagination.

JOAN. Of course. That is how the messages of
God come to us.

The end of Scene I is, in reality, the end of all the
scenes, for those who are brought into contact with
Saint Joan are never able to describe exactly what she
was. All they can say, and they say it over and over
again, is " There is something about her." It is
what is said and has been said ever since the romantic
affair on Calvary——There was something about
Him. Robert, how splendidly is he drawn by Shaw,
is never convinced by all that Joan says, by all her
seemingly absurd ambitions, but he is quite suddenly
convinced that there is something unusual about Joan
because, since he has acceded to her wishes, the barren
hens have laid five dozen eggs.

ROBERT. Christ in Heaven! She did come from
God.

I do not think that there is any need to waste any
time discussing the reason or otherwise that Shaw
allows Joan to address the Dauphin as Charlie and
speak to him in the accents of somebody we can only
describe as a yokel. Joan was a peasant girl ; she is
impressed by nobody. The Dauphin is merely a
rather unfortunate little man who hasn't yet got his
crown. He is a little bit unhappy because he has

not got his box of soldiers ; he is a little untidy. At present he has not the making of a king. Joan merely sees him almost as a little boy she is going to mother and put in his right place. It is she who will crown him in Rheims. It is she who tells him that he is to be the king of France. But not yet. At present he is Charlie and she is Joan. And Shaw is showing us a country girl talking quite naturally to the man she is going to work for. And also Joan must approach the Dauphin with a show of equality. It is quite obvious that he is reluctant to believe in her till he knows her well, and this can only be accomplished by Joan being perfectly natural and treating him as woman to man.

It is not necessary to consider the whole of Shaw's *Saint Joan*. It will be sufficient to deal with the last scene in the play, perhaps the best act Shaw has ever written, the trial of Joan by the Inquisition for heresy, that deadly sin before which even the Church might well quake.

.   .   .   .   .

In dealing with Joan's trial even the most superficial observer could not but observe the tremendous efforts that Shaw has made to be fair. And it is no small merit when there is no good disguising the fact that as a whole Shaw is ever inclined to be hostile to the Church. He does not in any way " use " the Church to make Joan more splendid than she is, nor does he represent the Church as a mere tyrannical monster simply ambitious for tyranny, simply a vast autocratic machine treading down the individual,

But the Church simply cannot tolerate heresy.   That
is the essential point of view of the Church.   Joan
cannot bow to the judgment of the Church if she feels
she is the recipient of a more efficient revelation from
outside.   That is the essential position of Joan.   The
clash is the trial, and Shaw tries terribly hard (and
succeeds) in giving a fair presentation of both points
of view.

The pride of the Church has ever been a position
hated by the world.   It is that pride which is not the
pride of conceit but the pride of possession.   Cauchon
puts it extraordinarily well when he remarks that the
Church is not subject to any kind of political necessity.
If the Church adjudicates Joan guiltless, she is guiltless.   If the Church adjudicates her guilty, she is
guilty.   There is no court of appeal.   The Church is
the last word, her finding is final, her judgment, the
judgment of the Vicar of Christ, is infallible.   But yet
in some indefinable way the Church is cunning.   Joan
shall condemn herself, she shall utter her own death
sentence, she shall give the Inquisitor quite an easy
job, she shall make him appear to be not only fair (as
he is) but generous (as he is in so far as his office will
let him).   Joan is indeed an invincible ally in the
battle to save her soul, the almost certain corollary
of which will be the burning of her body.

> THE INQUISITOR. You need have no anxiety about
> the result, my lord.   You have an invincible ally
> in the matter : one who is far more determined
> than you that she shall burn.
>
> WARWICK. And who is this very convenient par-
> tisan, may I ask ?

THE INQUISITOR. The Maid herself. Unless you
put a gag in her mouth you cannot prevent her
from convicting herself ten times over every time
she opens it.

Nothing in history has been more misunderstood
than the Holy Inquisition. Nothing can really justify
its existence. Nothing also can justify the attacks on
it as a mere piece of barbarous ecclesiastical machinery. It was quite simply an instrument of a Church
which hated heresy above all things, not because it
threatened to undermine the foundations of the
Church but because it was thought to bring the most
grievous damage to the soul of the heretic. Let his
body be *burned* that his soul be saved—so dogmatised
the ancient Church. Let his body be *persuaded* that
his soul be saved—so dogmatises the modern Church
or rather the ancient Church more enlightened. So
the Inquisitor apologises for his office and Shaw seems
to have penned the right apology. At the end of a
very long oration the Inquisitor concludes—" I am
compassionate by nature as well as by my profession ;
and though the work I have to do may seem cruel to
those who do not know how much more cruel it would
be to leave it undone, I would go to the stake myself
sooner than do it if I did not know its righteousness,
its necessity, its essential mercy."

Only a dramatist possessed of genius would think
of inserting in the middle of Joan's trial a human
incident which might be quite absurd if it were not
probably quite an accurate picture of what did
happen. There is nothing absurd in introducing into
Joan's trial something which shows that the Inquisitor

and the Bishop of Beauvais were something more than mere officials of an ecclesiastical judicial enquiry. The lines are worth quoting simply because they show how careful Shaw is all the way through this play not to write a play that is a mere historical play but a play that is history. It has always to be remembered that, like nearly everyone else, the Inquisitor and the Bishop of Beauvais were intrigued by the French peasant girl, who had crowned the Dauphin king in the cathedral at Rheims. This little incident of the bad fish that makes Joan look pale is not by any means the smallest attribute that helps to the brilliance of Shaw's play.

> THE INQUISITOR. Sit down, Joan. You look very
>   pale to-day. Are you not well?
> JOAN. Thank you kindly; I am well enough. But
>   the Bishop sent me some carp, and it made me ill.
> CAUCHON. I am sorry. I told them to see that it
>   was fresh.

The whole central position at Joan's trial is that she will accept the authority of the Church so long as the Church does not command her to do anything that she considers impossible. Therefore by a system of quite reasonable logic, the Church can quite well retort to her that she is a heretic because she implies that the Church may commit error and folly by commanding the impossible. She goes farther: she suggests, as hundreds and thousands of people have suggested who dislike subscribing to the position that the Church is infallible and therefore unable to order anything that might be contrary to God's command, that she can conceive of a situation (I think a theoretical one) in which she would not be able to obey the commands of the Church because she would consider them contrary to the command of God. The position is really a simple one and it is one that Shaw brings out clearly enough. Joan condemns herself because she relies on private judgment in matters that could only be settled by the judgment of the Church. To say, then, as Joan does, that the Church might command her to do something contrary to the Divine command is as rank heresy as to say that there was a time when Christ did not exist or that the first and second and third Persons of the Trinity are not equal in essence. Joan again condemns herself and it is most important, if we are to understand the absolute determination of the trial, by a hypothetical suggestion. That is that there may be a possibility of the Church erring in telling her to do something to which she could not in her own opinion subscribe. So she puts very clearly just how far she will go in her obedience to the Church and just when she may feel it her duty to substitute for the Church's judgment her own private judgment. But this is again of supreme importance. Joan will not substitute her own judgment for the judgment of the Church because she considers her own judgment is superior to the judgment of the Church, but because she discerns the possibility when the judgment of the Church may fail to be the actual interpretation of the will of God. Thus does Joan enunciate a deplorable and shocking heresy, a heresy that, allowed to go unchecked, would hurl the Pope from the Vatican, bring down St.

Peter's to the earth, snatch with stealthy violence the keys from St. Peter, make the infallible Church a laughing-stock and a scapegoat. The assertion by Joan that she may consider disobeying the Church and the effect of the assertion on the Inquisitors is written with astounding accuracy by Shaw. So in a really desperate effort to prevent Joan from finally condemning herself by her obstinate heresy, Ladvenu endeavours to persuade Joan that the Church and God and God and the Church are one. To which Joan replies once again that though the Church must be obeyed, God must be served first.

LADVENU. You do not know what you are saying, child. Do you want to kill yourself? Listen. Do you not believe that you are subject to the Church of God on earth?

JOAN. Yes. When have I ever denied it?

LADVENU. Good. That means, does it not, that you are subject to our Lord the Pope, to the cardinals, the archbishops, and the bishops for whom his lordship stands here to-day?

JOAN. God must be served first.

D'ESTIVET. Then your voices command you not to submit yourself to the Church Militant?

JOAN. My voices do not tell me to disobey the Church; but God must be served first.

CAUCHON. And you, and not the Church, are to be the judge?

JOAN. What other judgment can I judge by but my own?

There is but one more point that need be considered
in this play. Shaw has been much criticised for his
epilogue. It has been condemned as an anti-climax
by critics who do not see that the play does not rightly
end with the burning of Joan. If it did, then Joan
was merely a military genius not necessarily endowed
with any supernatural powers. The last lines in the
actual play might explain to the average dramatic
critic that Shaw never meant the earthly end of Saint
Joan to be the end of the play. You cannot get
away from it, Shaw seems to say, Joan will keep
cropping up. So at the end of Scene VI, when Joan
has been burnt and the excellent public have been
satisfied for the moment, the executioner, as excellently unintelligent as all executioners are, makes the
kind of dogmatic remark that we should expect from
a stable-boy or a cavalry subaltern! Warwick, who
happens to be slightly less unintelligent than the
executioner, will not agree with the superficial dog-
matism of the executioner.

THE EXECUTIONER. Her heart would not burn, my
lord; but everything that was left is at the
bottom of the river. You have heard the last
of her.
WARWICK. The last of her? Hm! I wonder!

That is just the Shavian point. The burning of
Joan of Arc is the beginning of her history. It was
obviously necessary that the play should suddenly
leave off being historical and become imaginative.
Whether the epilogue is good from the point of view
of dramatic art does not perhaps matter much. I

think it is good. I think it is good because Joan, indulging in conversation when she has become a spirit, talks so sensibly that there is no question of this epilogue being a mere kind of subtle propaganda for spiritism. All the dead people who come back are very much alive. Joan retorts to the King of France's absurd suggestion that she is a ghost by asking him how on earth a burnt-up girl can become a ghost. The Bishop of Beauvais is quite reasonably annoyed that, having been a bishop in the body, he finds his body has been dug up and flung into a common sewer.

The epilogue contains some of the best writing in the play, particularly when Joan has been canonised and all those who had condemned her kneel at her feet, but even so she finds disappointment. Men will cherish her memory but they do not want her back. A live saint would be too uncommercial. Men may cherish the memory of Christ but they do not want Him back. He would have too much contempt for all our values. And at the last line in the play Joan asks the old question : When will the world be able and willing to receive the saints of God ? It is Shaw asking when will the world understand the true meaning of the Life Force. Joan goes back to heaven and the play ends, but Joan does not end. Her disappointment may continue for a long time but it will not continue all the time.

JOAN. O God that madest this beautiful earth, when will it be ready to receive Thy saints? How long, O Lord, how long ?

When Bernard Shaw wrote *Saint Joan* he had arrived at the age when he might be expected to write a good play. He could hardly have been expected to write a magnificent play, and yet the unexpected is ever what we must expect from Shaw. With *Saint Joan* Shaw enlarged his dramatic art and added to it the art of the poet. The poetry of *Saint Joan* is that poetry which is the result not of verse but of an admirable combination of toleration and understanding. The play is a complete harmony : it is free from the biting Shavian satire seen in plays like *Arms and the Man, Candida,* or *The Doctor's Dilemma.* Although Shaw deals carefully with the intellectual position of the Church he does not necessarily attack it or defend it. He is the observer and interpreter of an historical event. All the characters in the play are drawn carefully. There is one outstanding characteristic of them—they are not in any sense Shaw speaking. That is, perhaps, the supreme difference between this play and other of his plays. Most of Shaw's plays preach Shavianism : *Saint Joan* preaches Saint Joan.

At the age of nineteen Joan of Arc was burnt. At the age of nearly five hundred Joan became Saint Joan. Nearly five hundred years after the death of Joan, Shaw wrote of the romance of her life and death. Wherever the Catholic Church is, there is to be found a monument to this one of the latest of her Saints. There are other memorials : those that stand in the midst of the crowds of working French people ; there are those memorials which are merely her bare history in bare history books. The memorial that

228 THE SUBTLETY OF G. B. SHAW

Shaw has raised to her by *Saint Joan* is no ill-fitting memorial to the French girl who rode at the head of the armies of France and now rides ahead in the armies of God.

Chapter IV

BERNARD SHAW TO-DAY AND TO-MORROW

THE most probable perplexity that many people feel regarding Bernard Shaw is whether he is really serious or laughing up his sleeve. The problem can be solved with the greatest ease. Shaw is always perfectly serious in what he writes. The probable reason why so many people think Shaw is flippant is that they mistake satire for mere cynicism, irony for literal expression. But that is only part of the reason. If Shaw is not taken seriously it is quite often his own fault. The public has long grown to expect Shaw to amuse and irritate by sallies of wit which are not so rude as they look. Thus, for instance, when Shaw is invited to a dinner and retorts he does not eat dinner himself and does not care to watch other people doing nothing else for three hours, it is alleged that he has rudely snubbed a courteous gesture of the spokesman of a dinner committee. He has done nothing of the sort. What he means is— I do not want to accept your hospitality and give you in return a mere polite bored interest in your whole proceedings.

Or again, when Shaw is asked to address a Literary Society which meets in the basement of a bookshop, he replies perfectly seriously that if he came the potential audience would become a massacre in its

efforts to become an audience. What Shaw means
quite seriously is—If I accepted your invitation I
should have to accept a hundred others and I see no
reason why I should specially favour you.

Or once again when Shaw is asked whether he
would consent to become the president of an asylum
for the sane in America, Shaw simply replies that the
whole office would be non-existent for the very good
reason that there are no sane in America who could
fill an asylum. This is not rudeness. It is simply
Shaw saying—for goodness sake, if you wish to waste
your own time with idiotic cultism, don't expect me
to be sympathetic. Shaw cannot tolerate for an
instant waste of time. He says or implies over and
over again that we must get to the root of things, get
to know the meaning of the Life Force, get behind
the wagon and push, burn our boats, build new ones,
but not new ones constructed by cranks for cranks.

The Shaw of the press is the false Shaw ; the Shaw
of plays like *Man and Superman* and *Saint Joan* is the
true Shaw. And the general public unfortunately
know the Shaw of the press, the Shaw the " copy " of
the gossip writer, the Shaw, the darling of the literary
gods. Of Shaw as the careful philosopher and
thinker they know but little. Publicity has made
Shaw and it has also made a Shaw who is more often
than not far removed from the brilliant playwright
who has honoured the English theatre by making it
the vehicle of his genius.

The little tale that I have tried to tell of George
Bernard Shaw is nearly told. I have but to sum up
a few of his special positions and ideals, and I have

to make some little attempt to suggest the future of
Shaw from the point of view of his right to immortality—the only immortality that Shaw would tolerate
—an immortality in the world of art.

. . . . .

Shaw would never be content to be thought of
merely as a dramatist. He has ever considered himself as a very practical philosopher. His whole life
has been a mission—a mission to fallen humanity.
Shaw started with the assumption that most people
were hypocrites and humbugs. No way of starting
life could be less likely to end in disappointment. An
unsuccessful episode of novel writing, and off went
Shaw on his life's work. For ever the theatre was to
be his home, for ever (but I anticipate) the theatre
was to house his plays, give shelter to his thoughts,
be the instrument of his genius.

The progression of thought displayed by the plays
has been an orderly one. Much influenced by Ibsen,
Shaw began to examine roads to happiness or roads
away from unhappiness. The magnificent Norwegian dramatist found no roads that avoided unhappiness and no roads that led to happiness. Such
a position was vastly unsatisfying to Shaw. The
early plays came along. There was *Widowers'
Houses*—concerning the pleasing little problem of the
clash of ideals and dividends. We know the result
that Shaw arrived at. Then he examined the
philosophy of a philanderer and found that it led
nowhere except to philandering. Mrs. Warren turned
up with her profession and all her beastly brothels.

Q

She had not found any road to happiness in spite of her admirable management of disorderly houses on the Continent, in spite of her charming marketing of women so that they might be kept for her clients. The early plays were just an examination of problems and there was no solution. But Shaw did not sit down and whine, nor did he sit down and praise God and ejaculate the pious little blasphemy—that we do not understand and we have no right to expect to understand.

Instead Shaw gritted his teeth, put on a very red tie, and got busy with more plays and began very definite attacks. London began to listen to Shaw— his strident anger could be heard above the jingle of the hansom cabs—his name began to be considered and people even did him the honour of beginning to dislike him. This upstart indeed—to upset our British complacency—how dare he attack the source of our dividends—how dare he write of those dreadful people who provide prostitutes for continental travellers. Shaw smiled—perhaps a little sourly —buckled on his armour still tighter—and out came some more plays—and along came some more British anger and a prophecy that this impertinent young playwright would have to be watched.

Arms and the Man, not by any means one of the best of the early Shavian plays, was a rather bitter attack on the army. It was all rather cheap and quite unfair. No one felt that Shaw knew anything about the army, and everyone has been quite convinced of that ever since. The play had its amusing points and now and again it was clever enough to

have been written by Shaw. But on the whole
it is a poor one and can be classed among the lesser
Shavian plays.

Shaw turned his attention to a clergyman. He
confused everyone by writing of such a possible
clergyman that there was a widespread opinion that
Shaw could not be serious. He was desperately
serious. He really did insist that clergymen were
quite often fine characters, that they did believe what
they taught, that they could grapple with a problem
and come out on top. The love affair between
Marchbanks and Candida was not by any means the
most important part of the play. The drawing of
Morell was. Having then written a play about a
modern clergyman, Shaw proceeded to *The Devil's
Disciple*. Here Shaw once again gets back to the
question of hypocrisy. The religious people are a
poor advertisement for their creed—those who are
irreligious are a poor advertisement for their creed.
The Plays for Puritans have one common and typical
Shavian standpoint. They are written as a witness
to the fundamental position—that revenge and
punishment are evils.

The Doctor's Dilemma finds Shaw indulging in a
heavy attack again. Doctors cannot be really sincere
as their living depends on disease. Shaw gets at a
half truth, a thing he is very prone to do.

We proceed to the essence of the Shavian point of
view as expressed in *Man and Superman*. Man is
governed by the Life Force and his failures are simply
his inability or in some cases his refusal to listen to
the expressed wishes of this Force. *Man and Super-*

man is the climax of the Shavian genius. Shaw never gets to such a high level again, although *Saint Joan* is not very far below.

The whole of Shaw's work after his assertion of the Life Force philosophy is of course an examination of man's blunderings in regard to the carrying out of it. The plays that are written previously to *Man and Superman* lead up to that play—the plays that come after seem more or less to lead down from it. The Life Force has an ambition for a Super Man, man must endeavour to support the ambition. The failure of man to do this is caused by the blemishes in him that Shaw attacks.

Major Barbara, an effective consideration of the Salvation Army, in some ways is chiefly important as being a discussion on that evil, which is for Shaw the greatest evil—the evil of poverty. All our sociological problems arise from it, it is the arch-criminal, the worst enemy the Life Force has to fight.

Getting Married is a discussion with a title that speaks for itself. Perhaps the main Shavian position is that marriage is immoral when the spirit of the thing has departed. Divorce must be by common consent and adultery might be the last ground for giving divorce rather than the first. In nothing is Shaw more right. Physical infidelity is quite without importance so long as mental infidelity does not accompany it. And quite often it does not.

Saint Joan, the climax of the later work of Shaw, as I have said, is the most un-Shavian of all the plays. It is a magnificent piece of drama, and conferred an honour on the English Theatre that produced it.

Saint Joan pleased the Catholics and Shaw might well have thought that his acceptance was complete.

Shaw is a good hater. He hates punishment because it is merely an argument in a vicious circle —Shaw has a profound contempt for those who practise cruelty to animals. He might well have this. *There is no more contemptible class in the world than those men and women who take part in cruel sports.*

Education for Shaw is hateful unless it includes a sound basis of economic teaching. Children must at an early age contribute something to the state. We can only trust it will not be an overdose of priggishness.

I have dealt at such length with Shaw's attitude to Christ and Christianity that I need only repeat his cryptic suggestion. Try Christianity and try to see what happens if Christ is really *alive*.

Certain plays I have not dealt with owing to the impossibility in a volume of this description of dealing with all the vast output of Bernard Shaw. Their omission has not been a mere coincidence but simply that I thought other plays more important for my purpose. *John Bull's Other Island, Fanny's First Play, You Never Can Tell*, and *Back to Methuselah* are all excellent in their way, but they can be omitted, in my opinion, more conveniently than any of the plays I have included.

We have now to consider very briefly the question of the future of Shaw. Any suggestions are put forward with the utmost diffidence and a knowledge

that literary or dramatic immortality is the most
difficult of all themes to discuss.

. . . . .

   Shaw, as I have already said in this chapter, looks
upon himself as both a philosopher and a dramatist.
It is surely quite obvious that he will not be remembered as a philosopher in the sense that he might be
remembered as the originator of a system of philo-
sophic principles. Shaw is a practical working
philosopher and we must leave it at that. It is in
the realm of the theatre that the real problem of
Shaw's immortality arises. Will his plays be among
those which can be classed as permanent? The easy
answer which said that some would and some would
not is only a part answer. It is not enough to say that
we might expect to find *Man and Superman* and *Saint
Joan* remembered and the rest gradually forgotten.
The further question does arise that we are only half
tackling the problem if we leave on one side the fact
that practically (I except *Saint Joan*) all Shaw's plays
are pure propaganda and purely Shaw's method of
preaching Shavianism. The complexity of the problem is that we have to determine whether the plays
in themselves have potential immortality *in spite of*
their very definite propaganda.
   The plays for the most part (I again except *Saint
Joan*) deal with modern sociological problems—
divorce, poverty, militarism, medicine, school education, certain modern cruelties as blood sports and
vivisection—and situations that arise from our
sociological position and our ethical standpoints,

They are then in the crude sense " topical " plays. We are then reduced to asking whether we are out-stepping the bounds of possibility in demanding that certain of these " topical " Shavian plays may come to be classed as immortal.

In other words we have to ask whether these plays are artistically meritorious enough to win permanent recognition. I am going to be bold enough to suggest that only two plays of Bernard Shaw can expect to be classed among those which are permanent. The two plays are *Man and Superman* and *Saint Joan*. As for the others do I imply from my position that they may expect oblivion ? I do not. I think that they will last " a long time." Some of course will quite obviously die when Shaw does, if they have not done so already. I refer to the little war plays, excellent as they were, and such plays as *Arms and The Man*, *Caesar and Cleopatra*, and *The Philanderer*.

Brilliant as so many of the Shavian plays are they seem to me to be so intensely of this age that their brilliance will not be quite enough to make them shine brilliantly in another age. I do not mean that they will not be read or even performed, but I do not think that they will be accorded a place among the plays that are ageless.

Having then suggested with extreme diffidence that only two plays of Bernard Shaw may expect a place in the literary universe for ever, it remains to ask why *Man and Superman* and *Saint Joan* will last for all time. There are, I believe, two reasons. The one that the plays themselves are written with that touch of genius that does not age, that touch of genius that ever rides in the heavens, that touch of genius which allows the written word to be enrolled among those written words which are immortal. The other is that these two plays touch on really fundamental problems—the Life Force that governs man and the eternal clash between the salvation of the soul and the destruction of the body. The other plays deal with important problems but they are mostly problems of the moment ; it may be that they are problems of the century. They are not, I believe, problems of all time. For *Man and Superman* and *Saint Joan,* as it were, sum up all the difficulties that occur in the other plays—man's use of his own life and man's loyalty and homage to God and the Church.

Again may I say that I think *Man and Superman* and *Saint Joan* will be retained for another purpose than the mere excellence of their art. They are a very definite picture of two things. The height of the Shavian art for making the theatre a pulpit, the height of the Shavian art of making the theatre the background of very great poetry.

In other words they will show to other generations what " Our Mr. Bernard Shaw " could do, and we do want those who come after to know the heights to which he could and did rise.

Once more I dare to prophesy that *Man and Superman* and *Saint Joan* will live while dramatic literature lives, that some of the Shavian plays will last " a long time," that the others will just fade away, having done their job of hitting things that needed hitting and hitting them quite effectively.

The life of Bernard Shaw has been a fight for the right. He has never hesitated to attack when he thought an attack was needed. Cruelty, tyranny, have ever been loathed by Shaw. He has not been afraid to attack men in high places or women in low places. Literature has rewarded him with the Nobel Prize and politics has awarded him with a dinner at the House of Commons.

Shaw has always counted it ill to be of good account with men who were of ill account. He has always refused to concede to popular opinion. He has always seen, far off it may be, that man was good. He has ever seen that man can do so much better.

The Shavian Superman is not yet. The proper understanding of the Life Force is not yet. We cry with Saint Joan—O Lord—How Long—How long—— And the answer comes from George Bernard Shaw. Sorrow, crime, poverty are with us but they are temporary. The new man that is to be already appears in the far distance ; his steps grow louder and louder, and one day he will be with us. And Bernard Shaw will be there to greet his Superman—the Man who accounts it only worth while to be up and doing that he may work not for his own purpose but for the universal purpose that the Life Force requires him to do.

BIOGRAPHICAL NOTE

THE City of Dublin witnessed the birth of Bernard Shaw in the year 1856. For the first twenty years of his life Shaw lived in Ireland. And then came the call, the call that comes to all literary men. He must go to London, the city paved with gold, so that the stranger walking along its persuasive streets may not step upon the bones of those who have found that the gold was a false gold. In London, Shaw wrote the novels that he called " The Novels of My Nonage." Fortunately they were more or less a failure. The failure made Shaw into a playwright. He has been one ever since.

The year 1884 found Shaw joining the Fabian Society. Shaw made a note of the year, the Fabian Society made a still bigger note. Shaw became a Socialist and Socialism ever since has been much bound up with what Shaw thinks.

From 1888 to 1898 Shaw spent his life as a professional critic. It was a little unnecessary to pay him for professional criticism as Shaw never began being a critic and has never left off being one. Three papers had the privilege of his services as a critic. They were *The Star*, *The World*, and *The Saturday Review*. Lest the public should take too seriously what he wrote in these papers, Shaw used a pseudonym that sounded like a musical instrument. He called himself Corno di Bassetto, a name that was an excellent disguise for an Irishman.

The year 1891 found Shaw publishing *The Quintessence of Ibsenism*. Five years later. having discovered that no road led to happiness and that no road led away from unhappiness, Shaw married, Miss Payne-Townshend became Mrs. Shaw,

Onwards from this date Shaw has written play after play. It has been very difficult to find any that have been unsuccessful. *Heartbreak House* was a bit of a failure. *Saint Joan* was the great success in the English Theatre in the early twentieth century.

The year 1929 saw the production at Great Malvern of *The Apple-Cart*. It produced a good deal of conflicting opinion. Those who praised it did not forget that any play that might be called " good " was an achievement for a man three years older than the allotted three score years and ten. Those who attacked the play as being distinctly inferior to classics like *Saint Joan* and *Man and Superman* quite forgot that a man does not at the age of seventy-three write a play that can expect to be classed with his best efforts.

Shaw loses no opportunity of 'aking part in public work. He still lectures for the Fabian Society ; he still attacks all kinds of things in all kinds of papers ; he still keeps people " guessing " throughout the world. Shaw is an old man who refuses to grow old.

BIBLIOGRAPHY

Widowers' Houses.
The Philanderer.
Mrs. Warren's Profession.
Arms and The Man.
Candida.
The Man of Destiny.
You Never Can Tell.
The Devil's Disciple.
Caesar and Cleopatra.
Captain Brassbound's Conversion.
The Doctor's Dilemma.
Getting Married.
Androcles and The Lion.
Pygmalion.
Overruled.
Man and Superman.
John Bull's Other Island.
How He Lied to Her Husband.
Major Barbara.
Misalliance.
The Dark Lady of the Sonnets.
Fanny's First Play.
Saint Joan.
The Shewing Up of Blanco Posnet.
Back to Methuselah.
Great Catherine.
Heartbreak House.

O'Flaherty, V.C.
The Inca of Perusalem.
Augustus Does His Bit.
Annajanska, The Bolshevik Empress.
The Admirable Bashville.
Press Cuttings.
The Glimpse of Reality.
Passion, Poison, and Petrifaction.
The Fascinating Foundling.
The Music Cure.
The Apple-Cart.

_____

The Nonage Novels.
The Quintessence of Ibsenism.
The Sanity of Art.
The Perfect Wagnerite.
Dramatic Opinions and Essays.
The Intelligent Woman's Guide to Socialism and
Capitalism.

_____

BOOKS AND PAMPHLETS FOR THE FABIAN SOCIETY

Biography of Bernard Shaw by Archibald Henderson.
Critical Studies of Bernard Shaw by Patrick Braybrooke,
G. K. Chesterton, Holbrook-Jackson, Horace
Skimpole, and J. C. Collis.